WE MAKE THE ROAD BY WALKING

Central America, Mexico and the Caribbean in the New Millennium

WE MAKE THE ROAD BY WALKING

Central America, Mexico and the Caribbean in the New Millennium

**Edited by Ann Butwell,
Kathy Ogle and Scott Wright**

EPICA's 30th Anniversary Anthology: Vol. II

The Ecumenical Program on Central America and the Caribbean (EPICA)
1470 Irving Street NW
Washington, D.C. 20010
(202) 332-0292; fax (202) 332-1184
email: epica@igc.apc.org
www.igc.apc.org/epica

An EPICA Book

Library of Congress Cataloging-in-Publication Data
Wright, Scott; Butwell, Ann; and Ogle, Kathy, Editors.
We Make the Road by Walking: Central America, Mexico and the Caribbean in
the Third Millennium / Scott Wright, Ann Butwell, Kathy Ogle
ISBN Number: 0-918346-20-7
1. Church and social problems—Central America—History—20th century.
2. Christians—Central America—Political activity. 3. Central America—Politics and government—1979- 4. Social conflict—Central America—History—20th
century. I. Wright, Scott. II. Title:

Graphic Credits: Prologue: Dennis Dunleavy (March for peace in Chiapas, Mexico); Chapter I: Jonathan Moller (Julio Cabrera, bishop of El Quiche in Guatemala); Chapter II: Dennis Dunleavy (Women in Chiapas, Mexico); Chapter III: Jonathan Moller (Indigenous women in Guatemala); Chapter IV: Dennis Dunleavy (Samuel Ruiz, bishop of San Cristobal de Las Casas, in Chiapas, Mexico); Chapter V: Dennis Dunleavy (Indigenous woman in Chiapas, Mexico); Chapter VI: Patrick Ahern (Children in Cite Soleil, Haiti); Chapter VII: Dennis Dunleavy (Grave of Basilia Gomez Lopez, 70, killed by a Mexican army attack in Ocosingo during the January 1994 Zapatista rebellion in Chiapas, Mexico); Chapter VIII: Dennis Dunleavy (Two girls in Chiapas, Mexico).

The Choice

I will remain with my people
the dispossessed
the deceived
the persecuted
the bargained-for.
With the people who have never been considered
human
but who keep standing up
and surviving
and beginning again....

I will remain with the ones
who have been three times dispossessed,
forced off their land.
The ones who've been chased like deer
through forests and jungles.
I will remain with the silent people....
who guard in the intimacy of their hearts
the last word.

I remain with the elderly,
with the widows,
with the orphans.
In the crushed hearts
of the weak
God finds strength.

Yes, I will remain with my people!

-Julia Esquivel
The Certainty of Spring

Table of Contents

Editors' Acknowledgments

To the martyrs and peoples of Central America,
Mexico and the Caribbean,
we give thanks.

To the authors of this anthology,
to Gary MacEoin for his support, and
to Siobhan Dugan for proofreading the text,
we give thanks.

To Phil Wheaton, founder of EPICA,
to Cathy Sunshine, Minor Sinclair, Margaret Low
and all former staff at EPICA,
to the Board of EPICA,
to the Editorial Advisory Board of Challenge,
to those who have so generously
contributed to EPICA,
and to Marilu MacCarthy, for helping
organize EPICA's 30th Anniversary Forum,
we give thanks.

To those who have remained faithful
in the work of solidarity,
and to our friends and families
who have been so generous
with their support and advice,
we give thanks.

To you, our readers,
we give thanks.

Introduction
We Make the Road by Walking

by Scott Wright

"Come right up to the front," said Bishop Murelli to me during a liturgy in Caxia. "Come up so that you can see the faces." They were above all, time and again, black faces, faces that shone—for moments, for a song, for the duration of a cry, a shout. And there were dreams, there were desires in these eyes— or tears.

Then I saw the other faces, the other eyes: among the peasants eking out the most wretched existences round the edges of Lima, above all, time and again, among the poor women, and above all—particularly at night—among the street children of Sao Paulo. I saw the eyes without dreams, the faces without tears, as it were the unhappiness beyond wishing.

And finally I kept seeing the faces of the Indians, faces shaped by the dark shadows of what is called the mysticism of the Andes. At all events, I, the European, would call it a kind of mysticism of mourning. In my view these mourning faces are shaped by a distinctive strength, a secret resistance.

Johann Baptist Metz

The faces of the poor tell us something—not only about their lives—but also about our own. A face reveals something about the relationship between the one who is seen and the one who sees. A face both reveals and conceals: it may reveal either joy or mourning—as in the story above—but it may also conceal joys and hopes, sorrow and anguish.

Metz asks a series of poignant questions: "Can we Christians in Europe [or in the United States] bear to look at these faces? Can we, do we want to, risk the change of perspective and see our lives as Christians, as churches—at least for a moment—from the perspective of these faces? Or do we experience and define ourselves exclusively with our backs to such faces? The temptation to do that is great and, unless I am mistaken, it is growing."

The stories and the analysis contained in this volume, *We Make the Road by Walking,* and its companion volume, *The Globalization of Hope,* are meant to be a response to Metz's question. Our conviction is that things are going very badly for the poor who make up the majority of the population of Central America, Mexico and the Caribbean. The global economy—and its current neoliberal model—is not working for them. Rather, it is creating a human disaster.

We are not naively optimistic about structural changes in the global economy occurring anytime soon that would favor the poor. But we are hopeful. Our hope is based on what we have seen and heard of the poor during the past three decades, on their courage, creativity and capacity to resist in the face of major oppression, and on the possibility to create alternatives—at least at the local level.

Local alternatives cannot be built and sustained, however, unless the global economic model of neoliberalism is challenged on every front, and the foundation for an equitable, sustainable and participatory model of development is put in its place. We need a globalization from below—from the poor—rather than from above.

At the Crossroads: Between Memory and Hope

Oscar Romero, the martyred archbishop of El Salvador, often said that we run the risk of becoming insensitive to suffering and death. In all of his homilies, he tried to make people see and feel the pain behind each death, and the value of every human life. Five days before his death, he spoke to a group of foreign journalists of the important role that they played: "You are the ones who bring the photograph of our people to the world. Help them understand our situation so that they might offer us their solidarity. Don't forget that we are people, and we are dying, fleeing and taking refuge in the mountains."

These words illustrate, in a direct way, the question before us. Why is it so important not to forget the massacre of hundreds of poor peasants December 11, 1981 in El Mozote, El Salvador? What does it mean to remember the stories of countless poor and humble indigenous families in Guatemala who were dying, fleeing, and taking refuge in the mountains and jungles of El Quiche during the 1980s to escape a genocide that cost the lives of 200,000 people?

Why bother to recall the drama of Haitian refugees risking their lives on the high seas to flee the brutal repression of a September 30, 1991 military coup that crushed their hopes for real democracy? Why think about the 45 indigenous men, women and children in Chiapas, Mexico who were cruelly hacked to death by paramilitary groups December 22, 1997 as they were praying in the village chapel in Acteal?

These are the stories that hit the headlines of major newspapers in the United States, when the drama is so great that it suddenly becomes "news" and merits our attention. War, refugees, massacres have the capacity to shock us from our daily routines, and briefly catch our attention. Sadly, what for millions of poor in Central America, Mexico and the Caribbean are matters of life and death, are for us a brief moment of concern, or sympathy.

But what about the stories of indigenous peasants in Chiapas, Mexico struggling to survive on a small piece of land? Or of young women in Port-au-Prince, Haiti, working 16 hours a day in a sweatshop for 16 cents an hour? Or of mothers and their small children selling tortillas on a busy street in San Salvador?

These stories do not usually make the headlines. At most they are "human interest" stories, or stories of the sad plight of the poor who do not fit into the global economy and struggle at the margins not to be excluded. Yet behind their struggle for survival, behind the suffering and tears, are global economic policies that are radically restructuring the way the poor live and die in the Third World.

Those indigenous peasants in Mexico are profoundly affected by the lowering of tariffs under the North American Free Trade Agreement (NAFTA) that allows the market to be flooded with cheap grain from Iowa. Those young women in Haiti are profoundly affected by the imposition of a World Bank plan to restructure the Haitian economy in accordance with the needs of global markets rather than domestic needs. Those mothers selling tortillas in the streets of San Salvador are profoundly affected by the lifting of price controls on basic goods like corn and beans making it even more difficult for them to feed their small children.

The broad and urgent concerns that we have tried to raise in this book by way of introducing voices and perspectives from Central America, Mexico and the Caribbean, from the poor, from peoples of indigenous, African and mestizo descent, and from women, bring us finally to ask: "What have we done for those indigenous peasants in Chiapas, Mexico? What are we doing now for those young women in the assembly plants in Haiti? What will we do tomorrow for those mothers and their small children selling tortillas in El Salvador?

A New Berlin Wall Between North and South

The world has changed dramatically in the course of the last ten years since the Berlin Wall was torn down. Suddenly, the Soviet Union disappeared from the map, Eastern Europe joined the West, and the major tensions between East and West, communism and capitalism, are a thing of the past. Today the West has triumphed; capitalism has no rival. But what about the poor of the Third World who are experiencing a deeper crisis of poverty than previously known to them?

The new international context is marked more by the dynamics between North and South than between East and West. While the Berlin Wall has been torn down, a new wall—called neoliberalism—has been erected between the developed nations of the North and the impoverished nations of the South. The dream of the poor in Haiti under President Jean-Bertrand Aristide has now become the goal to which the poor in Central America, Mexico and the rest of the Caribbean can realistically aspire: "To move from misery to poverty with dignity."

The challenge today is to develop alternatives to neoliberal capitalism and to eliminate the bitter fruits that it has produced: the exclusion of the poor, and the reduction of their lives to conditions of survival. The popular movements of the 1980s that struggled to transform unjust social, economic and political structures in society, today struggle to make a difference in the lives of the poor at a local level.

And make a difference they do. There are many inspiring stories of small-scale cooperatives, alternative health care and education projects, and revolving loan funds for women to enhance their ability to earn a family income. Nongovernmental organizations are picking up the pieces and filling in the gaps that privatization and deregulation are creating in the lack of social services for the poor. But the macroeconomic picture in Central America, Mexico and the Caribbean is grim, with no real hope for the poor appearing on the economic horizon.

Major cracks have appeared in the global economy as well. With the financial crises in Mexico, Indonesia, South Korea and Russia, "the global economic crisis" has made its way into the headlines. The tragedy is, if commentators in the North begin to speak of a global economic crisis, we can be sure that the reality of life for the poor under neoliberalism in the South is even more of a human disaster.

Option for the Poor in a Neoliberal Context

Behind what could be characterized as a structural crisis of the global economy and its contemporary model—neoliberalism—is a profound moral crisis of values. Churches throughout the world are beginning to call for the cancellation of the foreign debt, the elimination of neoliberal structural adjustment policies imposed on Third World nations by the World Bank and the International Monetary Fund (IMF), and for fair trade—with real protections for labor, the environment and domestic producers and consumers—rather than free trade.

In 1996 the Jesuits of Latin America released a powerful statement challenging the foundations of the neoliberal global economy: "We refuse to calmly accept that the economic measures applied in recent years in all Latin American countries and the Caribbean are the only possible way to orient the economy, and that the impoverishment of millions of Latin Americans is the inevitable cost of future growth. Behind these economic measures lies a strategic policy, an underlying concept of the human being and culture that must be discerned from the perspective of the models of society we aspire to and work for, at the side of so many men and women moved by the hope of life and of leaving future generations a more just and human society."

Xabier Gorostiaga, a Jesuit economist from Nicaragua, makes the point that real democracy in the Third World is impossible as long as pervasive conditions of poverty remain. "Real democracy is capitalism's greatest enemy," Gorostiaga says, because ultimately it leads to a democratization of global economic structures like the World Bank and the International Monetary Fund, something that the industrialized nations of the North will not readily allow.

In addition to a democratization of the global economy, Gorostiaga calls for a global alliance between environmental groups of the North and South, and empowerment of people who have historically been marginalized, particularly women and diverse cultures: "We need a world in which the biodiversity of nature will mix with the biodiversity of cultures."

Whether or not globalization is a good thing is not in question. It's on whose terms does globalization happen? Is it a globalization from the perspective of the North or the South? Is the underlying criterion what is good for the transnational corporations or what is good for the poor majority? Clearly an option for the poor would commit us to judge any global economic project on the impact it has on the poor, and whether it contributes to a model of development that is equitable, sustainable and participatory.

Liberation Theology in the New International Context

In July 1997, Third World theologians met in Sao Paolo, Brazil to share their concerns about the plight of the poor and the responsibility of the Church in the current neoliberal context. "We have witnessed deep transformation in the world scene, in the condition of the poor, and in the consciousness of the churches and theologians. We undoubtedly are living in a new human era with a global expression. This new era is characterized by the hegemony of neoliberalism and by the globalization of markets that—by their competitive, noncooperative nature—produce a devastating exclusion that harms the lives of the poor and the oppressed."

At the same time, the theologians recognized the tremendous challenges the poor of the Third World face in responding to their current situation of impoverishment: "The popular movements that were so vibrant and strong at the birth of liberation theology continue to exercise resistance, but they have also been significantly weakened, particularly in the area of labor organizations. Their projects are now fragmentary and they experience great difficulties in formulating alternatives to this new form of global domination."

The theologians expressed concern about the environment: "We see that the same logic that exploits the poorer classes and dominates poor nations, also devastates the Earth along with all its riches. To live an option for the poor today implies living an option for the greatest of all the poor—our Mother Earth whose very survival is being threatened."

They also offered new perspectives for their work as theologians: "It is important to recognize that new expressions of liberation theology have emerged in recent years—cultural theology, indigenous theologies, Black theologies, feminist theologies, and ecological theology. We wish to translate our option for the poor into a renewed liberating theological endeavor."

What hope, then, is there for the poor to create an alternative to the neoliberal disaster they live with each day? Gustavo Gutierrez, the "father" of liberation theology, responded to this question in an interview with the magazine *Vida Nueva* in Spain: "Our communities are going through a difficult, painful time, it's true. But pain does not signify that Latin America is not also living in a moment of great richness. The pastoral, social and political creativity of the poor of this continent is abundant. I dislike the extremes, but if I must choose between optimism and pessimism, I choose optimism. I have hope—as a human being and, above all, as a Christian—because our continent is very alive and the Christian communities are particularly rich, creative and fertile. I do not believe in historical determinism because I do not believe in the laws of history. I think that everything depends, in great measure, on what people do."

In a similar tone, another liberation theologian, Leonardo Boff, responded this way in an interview with the Jesuit Centre for Social Faith and Justice in Canada: "What characterizes Latin America is the great division between rich and poor. By far, the majority of the population are those who are forced to live on the periphery, those whose cultures are crushed, Blacks who are marginalized, and millions of workers who are oppressed. It was from this environment that liberation theology was born.

"Today, however, poverty is worse in Latin America than before. In the past people pinned their hopes on development; today we don't have that hope and we are even poorer. The challenge for the committed Christian is to not accept this situation, to say 'this cannot continue,' and to organize into groups, unions and political parties of the left to work for transformation. Let's not forget that we are the heirs of a political prisoner, someone tortured, someone who died on a cross and not in a bed from old age—Jesus of Nazareth."

The Indigenous Face of the Church

On January 1, 1994, an event occurred in Chiapas, Mexico that would transform not only the face of Mexican politics, but the face of global solidarity as well. In the space of a few hours, Zapatista rebels took over three major towns and declared their opposition to the Mexican government and its support for NAFTA. Suddenly, that which had been hidden for centuries—the indigenous reality of Chiapas—was now major news in newspaper and television accounts around the world.

Responding to this surprise, the Zapatistas said: "The people decided to rise up this same day to respond to the decree of death enclosed in NAFTA with a decree of life, and to demand the freedom and democracy necessary to bring about a solution to their problems. For we have to build a better world for everyone, and not for just a few."

Bishop Samuel Ruíz, the bishop of the Diocese of San Cristobal de Las Casas in Chiapas, responded to the rebellion with this confession: "From a global perspective, the indigenous peoples are the forgotten and marginalized peoples. They are strangers in their own land. This is the greatest social sin for which all of us should ask pardon. We cannot continue to build the Mexico of the future over the graves of indigenous peoples, nor can we ignore the most ancient roots of our national identity.

"It's not only justice that is at stake. In 500 years nobody has been able to eradicate the indigenous people from this continent. They are here to stay and they are claiming their right to participate. If you read the Zapatista declarations you will realize that by 'participation' they don't mean to participate on others' terms, but to offer what they have to give to the transformation of society in Mexico. The hour of indigenous people is beginning on our continent. This is their hour, not three days from now, but now. They are the womb of our continent."

Behind the Zapatista rebellion is a long history of oppression, as well as a more recent and fruitful collaboration between the Church in Chiapas and the indigenous people. Under the guidance of Bishop Ruíz, the Church began to listen to the cry of the indigenous people. In 1974, the first Indian Congress brought together representatives of 400,000 indigenous people in Chiapas to discuss their problems.

The representatives came with a series of demands: an end to land evictions; an end to timber concessions to companies—including US-owned corporations—that were clearing the Lacandona jungle and destroying the livelihood of the indigenous people; and the right to organize their own cooperatives. The government responded with more land expulsions and an army-led campaign of targeted assassinations and burned villages.

Sixty priests and nuns then met with the leaders of the Indian Congress and asked, "As people of faith, how can we help? What do you want us to do?" The clergy were told by the Chol, Tzeltal, and Tojobal indigenous leaders, "We want you to work *with* us. Look at our suffering. Side with us in our struggle for land. If all you have to offer us is empty catechism, nothing will change. But if you are offering us the Word of God, then put it into action."

The Church was transformed. Priests, nuns and catechists helped the indigenous people resist land evictions and form coffee cooperatives to better market their products. Pastoral leaders were trained in workshops that took place in their local villages rather than in San Cristobal de Las Casas. Priests and nuns learned indigenous languages rather than expecting the indigenous catechists to learn Spanish. The Church developed a pastoral ministry of incarnating the Word of God in the indigenous cultures "to bring a little bit of heaven to earth."

After the January 1994 rebellion, Bishop Ruiz agreed to serve as mediator between the Zapatista rebels and the Mexican government. Several issues have been negotiated, including the crucial issue of the right of indigenous communities to local autonomy. But since the December 22, 1997 massacre of 45 indigenous men, women and children from Acteal in the village chapel where they were praying, negotiations have broken down. Rather than negotiate in good faith, the Mexican government has sent thousands of soldiers to Chiapas to carry out a low-intensity war against the indigenous poor.

Women Transform the Face of the Church

As indigenous people were beginning to claim their rights to participate in society on their own terms, women were doing the same. Throughout Central America, Mexico and the Caribbean, women were not only participating in the struggles for justice—something they had done with great courage and sacrifice for years— they were also bringing a feminist perspective to those struggles and fighting for gender equality.

At the Fourth United Nations World Conference on Women in Beijing in 1995, a platform of women's rights was developed that addressed such issues as the feminization of poverty, i.e. the fact that poverty impacts women and children in ways that are even more oppressive than its impact on the general population. The statement reads:

"Absolute poverty and the feminization of poverty, unemployment, the increasing fragility of the environment, continued violence against women and the widespread exclusion of half of humanity from institutions of power and governance underscore the need to continue the search for development, peace and security and for ways of assuring people-centered sustainable development."

When we fill in the picture with the daily reality of a poor peasant woman in El Salvador, for example, it looks like this:

3:30 a.m. Wake up. Light the fire, clean the corn, wash the grinding stone. Grind the corn, knead the dough, make the tortillas, prepare breakfast for her husband.

5:00 a.m. Nurse the baby. Prepare breakfast for the children and send them off to school. Sweep the patio. Make the beds.

7:00 a.m. Eat breakfast. Feed the pigs and chickens. Carry water. Wash the dishes and tablecloth. Gather together the dirty clothes. Prepare the milk to make cheese.

9:00 a.m. Work in the cornfield. Prepare lunch. Gather firewood. Carry water. Light the fire. Wash and cook the corn. Wash the beans.

11:00 a.m. Carry lunch to her husband in the field. Serve lunch to the children when they return from school. Clear the table. Wash the dishes. Shuck and shell the corn.

1:00 p.m. Go to the river. Wash clothes. Bathe.

3:00 p.m. Return to the house. Hang the clothes out to dry. Prepare the cheese. Light the fire. Clean the clay *comal* on which the tortillas are prepared. Wash the grinding stone. Grind the corn. Knead the dough. Make the tortillas. Prepare dinner.

5:00 p.m. Serve dinner to the family. Nurse the baby. Eat dinner. Wash the dishes. Mend the clothes. Cook the corn for the morning meal.

7:00 p.m. Attend a meeting of the community. Prepare the children for bed. Pick up and arrange their clothes for the next day.

9:00 p.m. Go to bed. Get up during the night to respond to the children's needs.

This description of daily life is one that has not changed for generations. What is different, now, under neoliberalism, is that the future of agriculture as a viable occupation for the majority of the population is at risk. Globalization focuses the economy on producing for export, not for domestic need. Consequently, economic pressures are increasingly forcing the poor off the land and into the cities where they are left to fend for themselves in the global market.

A poor woman in the city must still feed the family. There are no pigs and chickens. There is no milk for cheese. She must buy water to wash her clothes. She must buy the corn for her tortillas. She must buy the firewood and buy the beans. Sometimes she must lock the children in the house while she buys these things, because they are not safe at home. Or she brings the children with her when she goes to sell tortillas and puts the baby in a cardboard box on the sidewalk to sleep.

What, then, can be done to change this situation? The Beijing platform concludes: "The participation and leadership of the half of humanity that is female is essential to the success of the search [for people-centered sustainable development]. Therefore, only a just and equitable social and economic order, and a radical transformation of the relationship between women and men to one of full and equal partnership, will enable the world to meet the challenges of the 21st century."

Women's participation and gender issues have also become important issues in the work of Christian base communities, Biblical reflection groups, and liberation theology itself. Ivone Gebara, a Brazilian theologian, captures this transformation as she relates her own journey from liberation theology to feminist theology to a gathering of women called the "Shared Garden": "What does being a feminist mean to me? It means to enter into a deep and concrete search for liberation; seeing the faces of those in need of liberation. My feminism and my theology try to be connected to the interests of the marginalized population, especially women and children. They are living without any social security, outside that system, trying to survive everything. Their lives are a real miracle."

Defending the Rights of the Poor

During the postwar period of the 1990s, another important struggle emerged that was centered on telling the truth about the human rights violations that occurred in the past. In Nicaragua, tens of thousands of civilians were killed by the *Contra* attacks of the 1980s. In El Salvador and Guatemala, the number of civilians killed by brutal military governments was even higher: 75,000 in El Salvador and 200,000 in Guatemala. The United Nations sent Truth Commissions to El Salvador, Guatemala and Haiti to investigate the past and put closure on the human rights violations that occurred under military governments in those nations. The Churches were also active in investigating and defending human rights both during and after the wars in Central America and the military coup in Haiti.

One such project of the Church in Guatemala is the Recovery of the Historic Memory (REMHI) project. In April 1998, REMHI published a four volume report on the massacres, assassinations and disappearances that occurred during the past three decades. Most of the violations refer to an intense period of military repression, bordering on genocide, carried out in 1980-1982 under Generals Lucas García and Ríos Montt, during which time hundreds of massacres against the indigenous population occurred. The April 1998 assassination of Bishop Juan Gerardi, the director of the project, only underscores the unfinished work of human rights in Guatemala.

Now that the wars in Central America have ended, and neoliberalism has taken hold as the dominant factor in determining the condition of people's lives, a new concern has emerged: poverty as a violation of human rights. This is a much more difficult problem to get a hold on, since decisions determining the global economy have been made with virtual impunity, both by governments as well as by transnational corporations. Today, the causes of poverty are being directly challenged. For example, churches and non-governmental coalitions throughout the world have begun to call on the World Bank and the IMF to end their policies of restructuring Third World economies to pay the foreign debt. Calls to cancel the debts of the world's poorest nations by the year 2000 are rising.

In December 1998, the world will celebrate the 50th anniversary of the United Nations Universal Declaration of Human Rights. One of the major debates in 1948—that broke down along East/West lines—was over social, economic and cultural rights versus civil and political rights. Fortunately, the declaration contains both, providing a rationale for regarding poverty as a violation of human rights.

Haiti is a clear example of economic decisions made by the World Bank and the IMF, and endorsed by the United States, that directly impoverish the poor. The World Bank's structural adjustment program has had a devastating impact on the poor in Haiti, putting pressure on small farmers to produce for export rather than for domestic consumption, or risk having to abandon agriculture altogether and seek employment in the growing assembly sector in Port-au-Prince. It's the same story repeated around the globe, but with even more dire consequences in a country as impoverished as Haiti.

Besides civil and political rights—and social, economic and cultural rights—there are also the rights of nations to self-determination and sovereignty. In this last area we include the concerns of the Panamanian people that the United States return the Panama Canal to them by the year 2000—in accordance with the Carter-Torrijos Treaty signed in 1977; and the concerns of the Cuban people and the Cuban Churches to end the 37-year-old US economic blockade of Cuba.

This latter concern was voiced most eloquently by Raúl Suárez, a Cuban Baptist pastor, founder of the Martin Luther King Center in Havana, and a deputy in the Cuban National Assembly. "Convince me," he old an EPICA delegation in 1995, "show me in the Bible how policies to blockade a country, to make a people weak with hunger, to make them rebel against their government, show me how this is just."

The January 1998 visit of John Paul II to Cuba only underscores this concern. The Pope has frequently called for an end to the blockade, supporting an earlier position taken by the Cuban Catholic Church as far back as 1969. In addition, John Paul II offered a strong critique of neoliberalism during his 1998 visit to Cuba:

"From its centers of powers, neoliberalism often places unbearable burdens upon less favored countries. Hence, at times, unsustainable economic programs are imposed on nations as a condition for further assistance. In the international community, we thus see a small number of countries growing exceedingly rich at the cost of the increasing impoverishment of a great number of other countries; as a result the wealthy grow ever wealthier, while the poor grow ever poorer."

Solidarity for the New Millennium

What, then, is the solution to the global problem of poverty that devastates the poor, particularly those sectors that have traditionally been excluded from society: indigenous peoples, Blacks, and poor women, youth and children? Global problems require global solutions. One such endeavor to find a solution is the "50 Years Is Enough" Campaign, a coalition of development organizations, churches, and human rights groups that directly challenge the structural adjustment and debt policies of the World Bank and the IMF. Already the debt of developing nations has reached the intolerable figure of $1.5 trillion dollars, more than the total of their combined resources. The nations of the North are literally bleeding the nations of the South to death, and women and children bear a disproportionate burden of the suffering caused by this debt.

The Jubilee 2000 Campaign is another example of a global effort to seek a global solution to the problem of the foreign debt. According to the tradition of the Jewish people, every 50th year a Jubilee Year was proclaimed, debts were forgiven and the land was returned to its original inhabitants. By proclaiming such a vision today, and calling for the cancellation of the foreign debt by the year 2000, the Jubilee 2000 Campaign is challenging policies of the World Bank and the IMF that cause great suffering among the world's poor.

Ultimately, however, global solutions to global problems will have to begin and end in the grassroots, in the daily lives of the poor who are most impacted by the global economy and who have the most at stake in the struggle to put in place global alternatives to neoliberalism. We need a global alternative from below—from the poor—not from above.

Another example of a global response to a global problem is the courageous witness and growing network of people across several nations who have organized to close the School of the Americas (SOA) in Fort Benning, Georgia. Founded in 1946 and based in Panama, the school was moved to the United States in the 1984 and became a center for training some of the most notorious human rights violators in Latin America. The school trained 19 of the 25 officers named by the United Nations Truth Commission as responsible for the November 16, 1989 killing of the six Jesuit priests and the two women in El Salvador. It also trained the National Guardsmen who raped and killed the four US church women in El Salvador on December 2, 1980. The list of SOA graduates involved in human rights violations is endless.

In November 1997, more than 1,500 people demonstrated in front of the school at Fort Benning, as 601 people crossed the line onto the base to be arrested in an action of nonviolent civil disobedience. Twenty-five of those who crossed were repeat offenders, and received jail terms of six months and a $3,000 fine. Four of their testimonies are included in this volume.

Another example of a global response to a global problem is the commitment of ordinary people on both sides of the US-Mexican border to defend the rights and dignity of Mexican immigrants in the United States. A few years ago, as conservative politicians clamored for more protection against illegal immigration, and fences were constructed to keep immigrants out, people from El Paso, Texas and Ciudad Juarez, Mexico celebrated Easter Sunday on the very spot where the fence would be constructed. Their message was clear: "Solidarity has no borders."

US immigration policy clearly reflects US foreign policy. In 1998, Cubans and Nicaraguans were granted political asylum, while Haitians, Salvadorans, Hondurans and Guatemalans were not. In addition to these countries, Mexican immigrants have never been granted the same favorable status as other immigrant groups from Europe or Asia. Yet it is precisely neoliberal economic policies that are driving poor Mexican peasants off of the land, into the cities and across the border. The close relationship between globalization and immigration makes all the more necessary a response of solidarity.

Every day along the border, that solidarity is present as families on one side welcome immigrants from the other side into their homes and communities, regardless of their legal status. Despite an ugly anti-immigrant sentiment in the United States that is periodically fanned by conservative politicians and media, there is also a real tradition of hospitality that functions as a form of resistance to unjust economic policies and rigid immigration laws. We include one story of many that could be told about people-to-people hospitality in this volume.

The Subversive and Joyous Memory of the Martyrs

We conclude our introduction by recalling the story told by Johann Baptist Metz at the beginning. The faces of the poor hold us accountable. They evoke in our hearts "dangerous memories" that cry out for justice, for truth, for a share of hope for the future. The temptation to turn away from their suffering is great. In order to resist that temptation, we need to join together and, in Metz's words, "create new forms of political life and new political structures to resist the massive suffering and mass death that has characterized much of the 20th century." Only political imagination and political action rooted in the memory of humanity's history of suffering and the witness of the martyrs offers us the power to resist the moral bankruptcy of neoliberalism in the present day.

So we must turn to the martyrs for strength, those who have paid the ultimate price. It remains for us to take to heart their example, and to give the best that we can to help lower from the cross the crucified peoples of the world. The only way to honor the memory of the martyrs is to commit ourselves to the ideals for which they struggled.

In the epilogue to this volume, Jesuit theologian Jon Sobrino speaks of "the subversive and joyous memory of the martyrs." The face to face encounter with the poor not only makes a claim upon our lives, it is itself salvific and offers us new meaning and deep joy. In Sobrino's words:

"Those who respond to the suffering of the poor often recover in their own life the deep meaning they thought they had lost; they recover their human dignity by becoming integrated into the pain and suffering of the poor. From the poor they receive, in a way they hardly expected, new eyes for seeing the ultimate truth of things and new energies for exploring unknown and dangerous paths. At the very moment of giving, they find themselves expressing gratitude for something new and better that they have been given."

And so we end as we began, with the stories and perspectives of the poor. If this volume helps to generate solidarity with the poor in Central America, Mexico and the Caribbean, we will be grateful. We do not expect that a clear path of solidarity will emerge after a single reading. We do hope, however, that the stories and analysis may provide bread for the journey. And we can take heart in the words of the poet as we continue on our way: *"Caminante, no hay camino. Se hace el camino el andar."* "Walker, there is no road. We make the road by walking."

Prologue

Facing The
New
Millennium

Hope On The Cross: The Crucified Christ Of The Americas

by Julia Esquivel

One of the most profound insights that have come to us from the past decades of struggle and hope in Central America, Mexico and the Caribbean is the conviction of Ignacio Ellacuria, S.J., one of the Jesuit martyrs in El Salvador, that the poor of the world are a "crucified people." Crushed by poverty and destroyed by repression, the poor manifest the face of the Suffering Servant. The Suffering Servant not only bears the wounds that injustice and exclusion have inflicted, but by these wounds we are healed of our blindness and complicity with oppression, and offered the possibility to walk with the poor and to struggle at their side for truth, justice and real peace in our world.
In the following article, Julia Esquivel speaks of hope born in the crucible of suffering. She is a Guatemalan theologian and poet. During the 1980s, she was forced into exile by the repression in Guatemala, and worked at the World Council of Churches in Geneva, Switzerland. She has written several volumes of poetry, including Threatened with Resurrection, *and* The Certainty of Spring, *published by EPICA in 1992. This article was first published in the Winter 1992 edition of* Challenge, *EPICA's quarterly magazine.*

Native people resisted the European conquest and rejected a European God who blessed the genocide of two-thirds of the indigenous population. But the image of a whipped, crucified and bloodied Christ profoundly penetrated the soul of the native people, especially of the women. This figure most vividly exemplifies the sufferings of indigenous peoples, not only during the colonial period, but scandalously even today.

The prophet Isaiah speaks in his prophecy about the Suffering Servant:

"Like a root out of dry ground, like a sapling he grew up before us, with nothing attractive in his appearance, no beauty, no majesty. He was despised and rejected, a man of sorrows familiar with grief, a man from whom people hid their faces, spurned and considered of no account (53: 2-3)."

The experience of the Suffering Servant, of being considered less than human, is familiar to the poor in Latin America. Five hundred years ago the humanity of the people of the Americas was a matter of doubt and theological discussion until the Church finally declared that the indigenous peoples were human beings. Nevertheless, the treatment which indigenous peoples have received throughout history has been anything but humane!

Hundreds of times our peoples have struggled to free ourselves, to exercise our sovereignty, to decide our own destiny and to create our own way of understanding and practicing democracy. But foreign intervention, particularly that of the US government, has impeded us. The US has used its enormous military force and threats of economic sanctions and blockades to subjugate us.

Examples abound: the intervention of the CIA in Guatemala in 1954; US intervention in the Dominican Republic in 1965, in Chile in 1973, and in Panama in December 1989; the war of aggression against Nicaragua and the Iran-*Contra* scandal; and a decade of war against the people of El Salvador. These policies have meant hundreds of thousands of people assassinated, disappeared, tortured, exiled and displaced, as well as increasing levels of poverty, disease and violence against our communities.

To keep Latin America in this situation of dependence, the industrialized countries of the North have designed "development" policies to exploit our raw materials and labor, impeding the freedom of millions of workers to organize and denying food to our people. Health conditions deteriorate, the poor are denied education, and the majority of our people suffer increasing misery.

The policies that the Western world has imposed on us have resulted in the concentration of power and money in the hands of a few. The face of poverty repulses the rich world of the North, and when the poor organize to defend their lives, the wealthy feel threatened and respond with repression. The insatiable greed of the "developed" world has disfigured the face of the Suffering Servant in Latin America and crucified our peoples.

Each day the number of unemployed poor increases, and families are forced to scavenge in the garbage in order to survive. We know from experience that neoliberalism will not change the unjust structures that cause so much suffering.

Creating Justice in a Situation of Idolatry

Despite the underdevelopment that has been imposed on us by the developed nations of the North, the great majority of our people continue to hope for a better life. Five hundred years of oppression have not diminished our faith in our Creator. We bear witness in our struggles and in our hope to our faith in a God of life who is also the God of the poor. We are becoming aware of the great responsibility we have towards the earth which still nourishes us despite the brutality to which it has been subjected.

Christians of Central America have discovered that working for justice is the greatest expression of love. Love is more than love for our family and friends. That is why the justice we want to establish in Central America must be founded on the dignity of the human person and, in a special way, on the dignity of those who are most impoverished and dispossessed by the capitalist system. The poor are not regarded as human beings by the rich and powerful.

God is life and gives life. Whoever believes in a God of life lives in order to give life. If the poor are not permitted to live with dignity, then we must be prepared to give up our lives as we struggle to restore the rights of our people.

In this world there are many situations of injustice that cause suffering and death, or make it difficult for the poor to survive. If we have faith in a God of life, we cannot permit this situation of injustice to prevail. Faith in God means rejecting idols, such as wealth and domination, that sacrifice the lives of the poor.

What does justice mean in a situation of such profound injustice? In the first place, justice means ending the impunity of genocidal governments like those of El Salvador and Guatemala under whose authority thousands of crimes have been committed by the armed forces, police and paramilitary groups. These crimes must be judged and those who committed them must be brought to justice.

Justice means judging the governments that accepted loans from the International Monetary Fund (IMF) and the World Bank that imposed conditions of economic austerity on our people. The terms of such loans were not agreed to by our peoples, and we should not bear the major burden for repaying them. The poor did not benefit from these loans, and we have been condemned to scandalous levels of poverty and to death just to pay interest on the debt.

Justice means valuing the lives of the people of the Third World as much as the lives of the people of the "developed" world. Thirty million human beings die in our world each year from malnutrition and hunger.

These deaths, which are the result of oppressive economic structures, are unjust.

Justice compels us to adopt the perspective of the poor in our practice of solidarity. This is the perspective from below, from the periphery; it is the perspective of those who suffer oppression. Only in this way can we recover the God of Jesus; only in this way can we begin to be Christians. The call to practice justice, which requires of us a concrete commitment of solidarity with the oppressed, is an occasion for our own conversion.

The struggle for justice opens our eyes so that we recognize the creation for what it is, our home and the home of all people, the source of life. When we struggle for justice we acknowledge the face of Christ in all human beings, especially in the poor to whom we are called to give life.

I

The Church
Of the Poor
In A
Postwar Period

Liberation Theology In The New International Context

by Pablo Richard

During the past two decades, liberation theologians in Latin America have demonstrated a remarkable capacity to interpret and illuminate the liberation struggles of the poor in their respective countries. Dramatic changes in the world have had a profound impact not only on those struggles, but on liberation theology as well. Twenty-five years after the English publication of his book, The Theology of Liberation, *Gustavo Gutierrez was asked: "In what sense has liberation theology changed in these last years?" He replied: "Our social and economic analysis has not changed. Poverty is still here and the situation has even grown worse. The globalization of the economy has meant that part of humanity is excluded from the world market. The poor are expendable. We have also been deepening our study of history from a theological perspective, giving greater attention to the contribution of indigenous peoples, Blacks, and women with respect to their cultures and their way of living out their faith. And we reflect on the Bible through the eyes of the poor.*

Pablo Richard is a Chilean theologian who teaches liberation theology at the Department of Ecumenical Investigations (DEI) in San José, Costa Rica. The following article was originally published in 1990 in an expanded version in PASOS, *a bimonthly publication of DEI.*

Many people in the First World think that with the end of socialism in Eastern Europe, liberation theology has no future. The dominant powers in the West have proclaimed the final victory of capitalism over any socialist model and declared movements for liberation in the Third World to be irrelevant.

This triumphant attitude, however, is contradicted by the brutal reality of poverty and oppression experienced by the majority of humankind. The conditions in the Third World that gave birth to liberation theology have not changed. As long as the scandal of poverty and oppression exists, and as long as there are Christians who live and critically reflect on their faith in the context of the struggle for justice and life, liberation theology will continue to exist.

What is most important, however, is not the future of liberation theology, but the future of the poor and the commitment of Christians to the struggle for life and liberation. We "do" liberation theology because of our option for the poor and our commitment to keep alive the hope of the poor for life. But liberation theology will survive only if we analyze the current international context and develop a theology that is faithful both to the original spirit and methodology of liberation theology and to the challenges of the future. We need to develop a theology that resists death and affirms life; one that renews our faith in a God of the poor and a God of life.

Liberation theology was born out of the participation of the Christians in the liberation struggles of Latin America in the 1960s and 1970s. It matured as the Church began to reflect critically on the faith and actions of these Christians on behalf of social justice. The theme of liberation theology has always been the revelation of God to the poor as a lived experience that is celebrated in community and reflected on within the context of the liberation process.

While traditional theology used Western philosophy as a basis for reflection, liberation theology uses the critical and liberating perspectives of the social sciences—including elements of Marxism—to identify the root causes of oppression and to reflect critically on acting to overcome this oppression in society. Liberation theology has never attempted to set forth a new theology, but rather a new way of doing theology—from the perspective of the poor and their struggle for justice and for liberation.

Liberation Theology and the Global Economy

In view of the crisis of socialism in Eastern Europe, capitalism is now presented by the West as the only viable economic model for the rest of the world. Before, capitalism had to compete with socialism in the Third World; now it has no competitors.

Capitalism no longer needs to maintain a "human face" or to be concerned about the development of the Third World; instead, a ruthless, totalitarian capitalism has been imposed on the rest of the world. The "New World Order" provides the United States with the rationale for exercising its political, economic and military hegemony to ensure that capitalism is accepted by all. The Third World has no recourse but to submit.

In the 1960s and 1970s, when liberation theology first appeared, capitalism had embarked on "development" programs for poor countries. Latin Americans critiqued this developmental perspective with their own theory of dependency, on the grounds that capitalist growth actually increased dependency on foreign capital and technology, increasing the gap between the rich and the poor. This laid the groundwork for a theory of liberation and the practice of revolution in the Third World.

The Poor as "Excess Population"

Under contemporary capitalism, however, a profound qualitative change has occurred in the lives of the poor and the oppressed. The affluent industrialized countries need the people of the Third World less each day. The First World needs the Third World's land to extract natural resources, to exploit tourism, and to dispose of toxic wastes. They may even need a limited number of people for cheap labor or as consumer markets. But the majority of the people of the Third World are considered "excess population."

To be exploited becomes to some degree a "privilege," since one is still part of the economic system. When the people of the Third World are excluded from contemporary capitalism, they lose all economic and political power. They cannot even exert pressure through strikes or boycotts because they are neither producers nor consumers.

Under contemporary capitalism, the powerful show little interest in the plight of this economic "underclass," whom they consider excess population. In consequence, there is little or no funding for services like job training, housing, health care and education. The deterioration of life is total and affects every sphere: economic, social, cultural and religious. This excess population is regarded by those in power to be "trash" or "vermin," something to be eliminated.

In some countries (such as Colombia and Guatemala) there are death squads that during the night kill street children, vagrants, beggars, prostitutes, homosexuals, the unemployed and the homeless. In other countries (such as the Dominican Republic) the urban areas are "cleaned" of poor people by forcibly relocating these people to remote areas and discarding them like trash.

The poor are considered a breeding ground for epidemics such as cholera, leprosy, tuberculosis and AIDS. The death of the poor and the oppressed is usually a silent one, and those who are affected the most are children, young people and women—especially those of indigenous or African descent.

Death or Life: Fundamental Contradiction of the Decade

The dichotomy of "development" vs. "liberation" therefore no longer adequately describes the current context of contemporary capitalism. The Third World is no longer dependent in the way it was before; instead it simply doesn't exist for the First World. The great majority of the people of the Third World are left to a situation of total poverty, abandonment and death.

We are no longer a Third World but a "Non-World," the cursed world of those who are excluded and condemned to death. Capitalism has largely abandoned its developmental programs for the Third World, pushing reforms only in small sectors of the Third World and only when this is in the interest of the First World.

Today the fundamental contradiction is not development or liberation, but death or life. Capitalism is an option for death; it bestows riches on a few people by exacting the death of many. In the present world situation, the option for the liberation of the poor becomes an option for life.

In this context, liberation theology becomes a theology of life. Life becomes the basis for a new ethic, a new spirituality and a new theology—all of which are radically opposed to capitalism in the current world context.

Liberation Theology and the Option for the Poor

In the last ten years liberation theology has expanded its concept of "the poor" and "the oppressed" to refer not only to economic condition, but also to race, culture and gender. The poor and the oppressed are not only those who are economically poor, but also people of indigenous or African descent; and women, especially Third World women who are doubly exploited—as poor people and as women.

Today we also speak about oppressed countries. The "Third World" (we use this term reluctantly, since we are not really a "third" world but the underdeveloped and exploited "two-thirds" of our world) includes not only the poor countries but also the poor of all countries, including the oppressed minorities in the First World.

The profound changes in the lives of the poor in the Third World radically challenge liberation theology in every way: its vision of the world, its commitment to liberation, its pastoral practice, and its ethics and spirituality. The preferential option for the poor requires us to commit ourselves to

40

defend the lives of this condemned and excluded majority in the Third World which is currently experiencing an accelerated process of deterioration and disintegration.

The struggle for liberation involves not only the interpretation of reality, but also a commitment to its transformation. We are challenged to create a new society where no one is poor, oppressed or excluded, and everyone has life and dignity. Liberation theology does not reflect on an abstract or universal faith, but rather on a faith that is lived in the midst of struggling to transform society.

Popular Movements vs. Political Parties

We will not try to examine all the changes in the struggle for liberation in this new international context, but only two that challenge the practice of liberation theology and call for a creative response. The first deals with the emergence of popular movements, rather than political parties, as the primary means of struggle for social change; the second deals with a shift in the form of struggle, from a military confrontation to a social one.

Popular movements in the Third World today play a leading role in the liberation struggle. That does not mean, however, that political parties are no longer necessary. Political parties and State power continue to be very important. The State should play a decisive role in the development of civil society, in economic planning and in the protection of the environment. The State, when it is stripped of its repressive apparatus, can play a positive role on behalf of the common good, the poor and the excluded.

In the current international context, however, the political power of the State is being challenged by popular movements more than by political parties. Leftist parties have tried to take power, electorally or otherwise, but they have rarely developed a radical critique of political power nor endeavored to create a new kind of power rooted in the majority of the people. Popular movements, on the other hand, instead of trying to take political power directly, work to create a powerful social base that has the potential of creating a new society. The creation of a new, profoundly participatory power is a major contribution of popular movements.

From Military to Social Confrontation

A similar shift has occurred in the form of struggle in the Third World, as confrontation becomes less military and more social. The struggle for cultural, ethical and religious values that defend the lives of the poor is not an abstract or ideological struggle, however, but a real-life experience that takes place within the popular movements in the Third World. This struggle is an essential part of the struggle for life and an integral part of the historic struggle for liberation.

There is a greater space for liberation theology to develop within popular movements than is possible within armed struggles. Likewise, liberation theology finds a privileged site for creativity and development in the cultural, ethical and religious struggles of the people. The current international context offers liberation theology a greater potential for growth and maturation and a challenge to consciously and critically respond to the urgent needs of the people.

Liberation theology has the potential to offer hope to the poor and the oppressed of the world. Its future, however, is inseparable from the future of all peoples on earth whose lives are threatened—and of the very earth itself. Ultimately, what is at stake is the life of the poor on earth.

The Church
Of The Poor
In Nicaragua:
A New Appraisal

by María López Vigil

*The defeat of the Sandinistas in the 1990 Nicaraguan elections sent a dramatic
signal to people both throughout Central America. Popular support for the
revolution could no longer be taken for granted, especially after a decade of
US intervention and economic aggression against the people of Nicaragua.
The moment was ripe to take stock of the new political context, as well as to
review past mistakes and make tentative proposals for the future. One of the
major supporters of the Sandinista revolution was the Church, although with
time sharp divisions occurred between the Christian base communities and the
Church hierarchy. The phrase, "Between Christianity and the revolution, there
is no contradiction," which had originated in Nicaragua soon after the
Sandinista victory in July 1979, was now in need of a new appraisal.
The following article was written by María López Vigil in 1991. She is a
theologian, the editor of* Envío Magazine—*a publication of the Central
American University (UCA) in Nicaragua—and the author of several books
and articles on the Church in Central America and Cuba. The following article
appeared in 1991 in* Amanecer, *a monthly publication of the Antonio
Valdivieso Ecumenical Center in Managua.*

When María Montenegro, a singer of wonderful children's songs, learned
the results of the Nicaraguan elections on the night of February 25, 1990,
she said, "We were touched by death." In the following months, I have not
heard any metaphor more expressive to describe what we all felt that night.
All of us who loved the Sandinista revolution died a little that night.

I use the word "death" not out of a sense of pessimism about what
happened nor out of exaggeration or masochism. I use it out of respect for

what we experienced that day, and also because in the light of death, we better understand life, what the life of the revolution was and what it tried to be. It is our hope that this death will result in resurrection. Politically, this means that the revolution will return to power and that we will rebuild what today there is an attempt to destroy.

In the light of the future resurrection of the Sandinista movement we will be able to better understand the defeat of February 25 and the full significance of the past ten years. We should remember that the Gospels were not written until after Jesus' death and resurrection. Only then were his friends able to understand his life and only then could they tell about it and reflect on it.

The Church of the Poor

I want to reflect in a new way on the life of the last ten years. I speak from the perspective of the Catholic Church, the Church to which the majority of Nicaraguans belong and the one which caused the most problems for the revolution. However, I want to analyze these past ten years from the perspective of the Church of the Poor, rather than from the perspective of the institutional church.

I think the first thing it is necessary to say—or to recall—is that in Nicaragua the Church of the Poor is weak. It was weak before the triumph and it was weak during the revolution. I say "weak" referring to the degree of organization, development, experience and tradition of the Church of the Poor; all this was weak in comparison with the Church of the Poor in other Latin American countries, including neighboring ones such as El Salvador. The development of the base communities and the assimilation of the theology of liberation were weaker here.

The triumph of the Sandinista popular revolution made the Church of the Poor appear stronger than it really was. As a result of the revolution, a responsibility to the continent, the world and history was attributed to the Church of the Poor, an expectation out of proportion to its strength. It was as though a child who had just begun grade school were expected to act like a doctor. What was barely a mustard seed with much potential, but only potential, began to appear in the eyes of its friends and enemies like a big tree, immense and strong, like a powerful beacon which illuminated nations.

For friends of the Church of the Poor, this was the projection of their wishes and dreams. How many people in the world wanted there not to be a contradiction between Christianity and the revolution! Because in Cuba there had been a contradiction and in Latin America there was no other experience to look to. Friends came from everywhere, from the East and from the

West, from the North and from the South, as in an epiphany, to see this church, to know it, to admire it, and to learn from it. There were so many people who asked, "Where are the leaders? Where are the projects? Where are the communities? Because we saw the star and we came." It was a question of too much clothing for too small a body.

Its enemies also misrepresented the strength of the Church of the Poor and converted it into something very dangerous. Faced with this threat, even the Pope took sides. He was the one who directly intervened in the most symbolically important issues: the suspension of the priests who held government office, the appointment of the Archbishop of Managua as cardinal. The Pope's visit in 1983 was a clear alignment with one side in both the church and the national conflicts.

The Sandinista Front also had an unrealistic conception of the Church of the Poor. At times, the Front believed that the Church of the Poor was much stronger than it really was and dragged it into involvements and positions that polarized the situation even further. On other occasions the Front tried to substitute itself for the Church of the Poor.

Within our church during those years, not having a supportive bishop and being estranged from the institutional Church contributed to weakening this model of church. The hierarchy's strategy prevented us from relating to Church structures such as parishes. We were dispersed and became disunited. All of these factors weakened us. The revolution and the great international expectations for it strengthened us, but the isolation from everything that is part of the tradition of unity and hierarchy within the Catholic faith weakened us.

Nicaraguan Popular Religiosity

I think that what most weakened us was the fact that we ourselves took for granted that in Nicaragua the synthesis between faith and politics had been achieved. However, this is a very difficult "marriage" to achieve. In the consciousness of the people, the step from an ahistorical religiosity unrelated to the reality in which we live, to an historical faith is a long and difficult process that requires constant pastoral accompaniment. The social convulsion that is an inevitable consequence of revolution is not the environment that best facilitates the rhythm of this process.

The religion of the majority of the people of Nicaragua is ahistorical. It has saints, churches and fiestas, but it does not relate to history, to everyday life, or to communities and the political and economic challenges they face. For the majority of the people, Jesus is a being from heaven, from outside the real world. He is the one on the altar, the one with long, curly hair. For the majority of the Nicaraguan people—and surprisingly for many Christian revolutionaries, too—this was their most basic expression of their faith, of the way they experienced their relationship to God. There was no synthesis, no experiential link between faith in God and Christian commitment, between love for the Virgin Mary and activity in the community.

We didn't recognize our situation at the time. We even thought that the synthesis between Marxism and Christianity had been achieved! Imagine thinking that the roof was in place when not even the foundation had been laid! We didn't realize that our task was to help people understand—and this requires time and education—that one's faith has a community aspect, that collaborating in a drinking water project is an act of faith and of love for the God who is present in our brothers and sisters. I say all this so that those who are not part of the Church of the Poor can see that it is smaller than they believed and so that those who are part of it will remember.

The Conflict Between the Hierarchy and the State

In addition to a weak foundation, our church was constantly in the midst of conflict. For years the Church of the Poor was caught in the conflict between the Catholic hierarchy and the revolutionary state. At some points, this was the conflict of greatest ideological importance in the country, much more intense than the conflict between the revolution and the political parties and businessman who today govern the country. At all times the Church of the Poor was deeply affected by this conflict.

If one looks at the events of those years and observes when the most intense moments of the conflict occurred and when the truces took place, it is apparent that the evolution of the Church-state conflict paralleled the evolution of the war itself. Seen from this perspective, the difficult relations between the revolution and our Catholic hierarchy have not been as irrational as some people believe; rather, these relations basically reflected what was happening militarily.

For the Sandinistas, the origins of the conflict stemmed not from their supposed antireligious ideology, but rather were due to a lack of experience in how to deal with religion and, still more, in how to deal with religion as a transnational corporation, one so dangerous and powerful as the institutional Catholic Church.

For the hierarchy, I think that the reasons behind the conflict essentially came down to two premises. First: the revolution is bad. That is, it is dangerous, suspect, atheistic, anti-Christian. Second: the revolution is reversible. That is, it is weak, it is not going to last, it is not going to be sustained.

The whole hierarchy-state conflict is understandable if we consider that it grew out of these two perceptions and the resulting struggle to overturn the bad and to reverse the reversible. To the degree that the bishops realized that the revolution was not as reversible militarily as they had believed (and even wanted), they began to develop positions that were less confrontational. Now they are at peace and happy: in the electoral defeat they see proof of the reversibility of the revolution. In light of the defeats we have experienced and of our hope of eventually governing again, we should begin a process of intense reflection and self-criticism.

As the Church of the Poor we have great responsibility with regard to how we speak and how we use God's word to conscientize people and help them reflect on reality. It is a great responsibility, because in the dialectic that we learn from the theology of liberation—of announcing the Kingdom and denouncing that which is opposed to the Kingdom—we Christians of Nicaragua were responsible for something new and unprecedented: proclaiming the signs of the Kingdom from within a revolution.

We had to proclaim the Kingdom within a people's army, within a popular government, and within the state structures that for the first time belonged to the people. This was a completely new challenge. Denouncing those aspects that were anti-Kingdom from within the revolution, within the army, and within the popular government was difficult. Not because of cowardice but because, faced by enemies who were so near and so cruel, it would often have been short-sighted and even destructive to denounce the negative aspects of the revolution.

Never before had the announcement/denouncement dialectic been put to a test such as this and we had no guidelines. In spite of these difficulties, however, and in spite of our lack of experience and the unique nature of the situation, I think that we should also admit that we lacked courage when it came to criticizing the revolution. Each of us should look at how we acted in this regard and decide when and how we could have criticized constructively, but chose otherwise.

Synthesis of Faith and Politics

Another error in our pastoral practice was one we have already pointed out: because we took for granted the synthesis of faith and politics as something already achieved, we skipped steps, we neglected the long, slow process of conscientization. We repeated the slogan "Between Christianity and revolution there is no contradiction," and this hindered us from seeing the contradictions that in reality did exist.

We Make the Road By Walking

There were many contradictions and these gnawed at people's consciences. What we were shouting was a theoretical slogan. What we meant by it was that we didn't want there to be a contradiction, or that there shouldn't be a contradiction. But, misled by this idealized and voluntaristic position, we didn't sufficiently recognize the real contradictions that existed, in order to be able to confront them and work them out pastorally.

Our language was very theoretical. At times the language of the popular church was accurate, but very abstract, very theoretical and very boring. It was very weighted with ideology: "the project of the Kingdom," "the commitment to the historical sectors and to the people as the subjects of structural change in the name of the incarnation of the Gospel," etc.

This kind of language doesn't say anything to people: not to their minds, which haven't attained a synthesis of faith and politics, nor even less to their hearts, which follow Saint Dominic as they dance in the procession on his feast day, or lead them to build an altar to the Virgin Mary, or to celebrate the fiesta of San Carlampio, making promises and drinking liquor. The majority of our people don't find warmth or meaning in this language, which only reinforces in them the impression that the Church of the Poor is nothing more than the religious branch of the Sandinista Front.

I remember a talk about Jesus that I gave in 1981 to a youth group in the San Judas neighborhood. I spoke about Jesus, an artisan with brown skin—not fair like in the movies, because he was Middle Eastern—with sandals, and sweaty. The young people who listened to me thought that I talked about Jesus that way because I was a Sandinista. In fact I was simply talking about Jesus of Nazareth, the historical Jesus, the only one, but the polarization and their lack of Christian formation made it difficult, even controversial, for them to accept this message.

Everything was polarized. Our theoretical and ideological language contributed to this, too. We didn't talk about real life; rather we theorized. This is a permanent error of "the left," including the religious left. We didn't talk about the Virgin, the Holy Spirit, or about heaven and hell. We didn't talk about the saints and their lives. We always talked about the "historical project of the Kingdom." But the people were more concerned about the question of whether they were going to burn in hell or not. They were interested in which saint was more powerful or performed more miracles. They were concerned about whether or not purgatory really exists. That is where we have to begin.

We should also recognize that it can be a great liberation for people to lose their fear of purgatory. In the past we refused to talk about such things, because we thought that these topics were vestiges of a declining, "alienating" religion, while we were working toward a "liberating" religion. We also misused Biblical readings, almost mechanically identifying the revolution with the Kingdom. In many of our meetings, we opened the Bible and interpreted everything that we read, whether it was Joshua or Deuteronomy or Ezekiel, as being fulfilled in Nicaragua at that moment.

Finally, I think we talked more about Cardinal Obando than about Jesus of Nazareth. We were more concerned about ecclesiology than about Christology. It shouldn't have been that way. We should have been more interested in "Jesus-ology," because the right way to build another model of church, a Church of the Poor, requires that we talk more about Jesus and about his message than about the Catholic hierarchy and its manipulation of the Church.

To the degree that the image in the people's hearts and minds of Jesus as distant, mysterious, and remote from the real world is transformed into an image of Jesus as a friend and a real person who was irreverent towards the political and religious authorities of his times, the people will come to question Church authorities when these authorities betray Jesus. The people will have in their hearts and heads the foundation necessary to freely question all authoritarianism which tries to impose itself in the name of God.

The Crisis of Communism

I think it is inaccurate to talk of a crisis of communism. Communism still hasn't existed. The crisis is only of socialism as it has been practiced. It is as if we said that there was a crisis of the Kingdom of God. No, when there is a crisis, it is a crisis of the Church, but never of the Kingdom of God, which is a utopia, the goal at which we want to arrive. A crisis of socialism as it has been practiced is more accurate. But "crisis" does not mean "end"; it can mean purification, new life. I think that no one has more of a right—and more of a duty, too—to struggle, to dream, to live and to die for socialism than Christians.

Socialism refers to a society that seeks greater equality among people. Equality amid diversity, naturally, but equality of dignity, of opportunities, of rights and of responsibilities. A society where no one has too much and no one has too little. A society without oppressors, who cannot act as brothers and sisters because they oppress others, and a society without oppressed people, who cannot live as brothers and sisters because they are oppressed. The kind of socialism we want is the kind Jesus preached in the Gospel.

I remember that when we were writing the book *Un Tal Jesús,* I asked that great Biblical scholar Father Juan Mateos how Jesus' "project" would be described in today's political language, how it could be translated into words that we know and use today. I remember he told me that the most accurate way to translate it would be as "anarchistic socialism." "Socialism," because it is characterized by equality. "Anarchistic," because of Jesus' permanent critique of power. We must struggle for this egalitarian and anarchistic socialism because it is critical and vigilant towards power, which always corrupts.

We believe in socialism because we believe that we are all children of God. But as long as those who exploit their brothers and sisters don't recognize this, it will be necessary to struggle against them, from above and from below, lifting up in this struggle the interests and the dreams of the poor, and loving them, not because they are good, but because they are poor, because that is how God loves them.

El Salvador: Death And Resurrection Of A Crucified People

from the Oscar Romero Pastoral Center

The Church of El Salvador, like the Church in Nicaragua, accompanied the people in their aspirations for justice in El Salvador. And the Church paid a price for its fidelity to the Gospel. Included among the 75,000 people killed during the war were hundreds of catechists, five religious women, 16 priests and Archbishop Oscar Romero. Just moments before he was assassinated at the altar on March 24, 1980, Monsignor Romero offered these words of reflection: "Every effort to improve society, above all when society is so full of injustice and sin, is an effort that God blesses, that God wants, that God demands of us... If we illuminate with Christian hope these longings for justice, peace and goodness that we still have on this earth, they will be realized... These deeds are not lost; purified by the Spirit of God, their effects are our reward."
The following reflection was published in the April 1992 edition of Letter to the Churches, *published by the Central American University (UCA) in San Salvador and translated by CRISPAZ. It appeared just three months after the signing of the Peace Accords.*

In El Salvador, as in many other places of Latin America, Holy Week is, for the majority, the most important religious time of the year; of Holy Week, the most important day is Good Friday, and of this, the most important moment is the Holy Sepulchre. It has been this way for years and continues to be so despite the efforts of officials, liturgists and biblicists to change things; i.e. to put more emphasis on the official liturgy than on the processions and to balance the meaning of the cross with that of resurrection. But this comes from far away—it is important to remember this as we also remember the 500th anniversary. And it will be good to learn the lesson it has to teach us.

Official Christology has moved to one side and real Christology—that of the poor majority—has moved to the other. Why? Because the poor and oppressed have identified since the beginning with the suffering of Jesus on the cross that has been associated with their own suffering, cruel and unjust, imposed and inescapable, which accompanies them from birth until death. This has been a true enculturation because the people of this land, who were conquered and subjugated by the conquistadors and pillagers, integrated the betrayed Christ in a very specific way: as a Christ who was also defeated and made to suffer. They could recognize this Christ and from him they learned the patience to be able to carry on with life despite the lack of dignity.

This is still true today. If in the Letter to the Hebrews it says that Christ was not ashamed to call his brothers and sisters those people who lived in countries like El Salvador, the opposite is also true. The poor are not ashamed to call Christ their brother. They are not only not ashamed, they need him.

This being so, the first lesson is this: We live in an unjust and cruel world in which the procession of the Holy Sepulchre, opiate or not, still expresses the most obvious aspect of our reality—people walking along the road accompanying a dead body. The wise should not be scandalized and the powerful should not make fun of the poor when they are seen walking behind a dead Christ.

El Salvador: A Crucified People

Many things have not changed with the passing of the centuries, but a message like that of Archbishop Romero and a theology like that of Father Ignacio Ellacuria, S.J., have accomplished two important things: to return awareness and dignity to the people. "You are divinely pierced," Archbishop Romero said in 1979 to the peasants at Aguilares, terrorized by the assassinations committed by the Salvadoran army during the month in which the people were surrounded by soldiers. "You are the crucified people, the presence of Christ crucified in history," repeated Father Ignacio Ellacuria. None of this changed the suffering of the people, but it offered them awareness and dignity.

A pastoral message and a theology that are today given to the poor and the oppressed who are crucified like Jesus and that explain the causes of Jesus' cross also tell the people who they are and why they are being crucified. And although there are many ways to awaken consciousness, this is a powerful way: "They are killing you in the same way that they killed Jesus: the sin of the world, the unjust structures, the idols of this world."

And it gives the poor dignity. It might seem like a small thing to those who enjoy the possibility of life, but it is a big thing for the poor to be told that they are the living Christs of today. And it is crucial to stress that they really are. The majority who die slowly due to poverty, or quickly due to the massacres of hundreds of old people, children, women—as happened in El Mozote or at the Sumpul River in El Salvador, as well as in Huehuetenango, Guatemala, in Ethiopia, in Haiti, in the Sudan—they reproduce the cross of Jesus today.

They are innocent, for they have done nothing to deserve death except to be poor and to be defenseless against their executioners. They are the ones who unjustly carry the sins of those who have been slowly annihilating them in life and definitively in death. They express the innocent suffering of this world. And, without asking for or knowing it, they complete in their flesh what is still lacking in the passion of Christ.

Thus, the second lesson: To pursue the real *via crucis* is not just an image of what passes in the street on Good Friday, but the image of a whole people being crucified. The difference is that they now know it and that gives them dignity.

El Salvador: A Resurrected People

It is not easy to speak of the people of El Salvador as resurrected and, in some cases, we cannot do so in the same way that we speak of them as being crucified as though the two things were symmetrical. We should also not appeal to cheap rhetoric that will surely be exposed by history. But we also cannot ignore the theme, from a Christian point of view, for our faith would be in vain if there were nothing of resurrection in our history. And from a historical point of view, it would be difficult for us to speak with responsibility and credibility if we offered nothing of resurrection to the poor along with the obvious event of the cross. The question, then, is: What is there of resurrection in our history?

That the Peace Accords have prevented war these past three months is already evidence of resurrection in our country—and the greatest of its signs. It is, however, not enough, as simple survival continues to be the major difficulty of a majority of Salvadorans. It is not possible, then, to claim victory but one also cannot deny another important sign of resurrection. In this work of making life possible, the Salvadoran people have developed signs in history that express what in resurrection is the victory over negativity and death. In other words, it expresses what is possible—because it is real—in living as a resurrected people.

No one has yet succeeded—although many have tried—in taking away from the Salvadoran people the hope that life, justice and reconciliation are possible. They have not taken away the freedom and love to decide to work, to struggle, to even give life itself for the well-being of others. They have not taken away the joy and the capacity for celebrating the small or great triumphs, the small or great feats of creativity, the way of living as brothers and sisters in community.

As we said earlier, it is important to be honest. Quantitatively in our country, there is more of the cross than of resurrection. But qualitatively, one can also not ignore what there is of hope, of freedom, of sacrifices, of joy and of celebration. And—this is the third lesson—when all of these things are real there is also resurrection. What we have learned in these years in El Salvador is that the miracle of God is transcendent resurrection and the miracle of God is also living in history as a resurrected people. Life continues to have the last word and this, more than anything, is what we celebrate during Holy Week.

The Mission
Of The Church
In Postwar
Guatemala

from the Guatemalan Churches

In December 1996, the Guatemalan government and the Guatemalan National Revolutionary Unity (URNG) signed the Peace Accords that formally put an end to more than three decades of fighting. During that time, more than 150,000 people were killed, and 50,000 were forcibly detained and disappeared. More than 440 indigenous villages were razed to the ground during an intense period of repression in the early 1980s bordering on genocide. Like the Church in El Salvador, the Church in Guatemala was also inserted in the struggle of its people for justice. It, too, paid a cost, with the assassination of hundreds of catechists, eighteen priests and most recently, the killing of Bishop Juan Gerardi.
The following declaration was issued following the signing of the Peace Accords. It was authored by the Guatemalan Conference of Religious (CONFREGUA), the Foundation for Peace and Reconciliation, the Social Department of the Archdiocese of Guatemala, and other church organizations. It was published in CRIE, *in Mexico, in November 1997.*

The signing of the Peace Accords on December 29, 1996 was an important step in Guatemalan history. That day the door was opened to move towards a different kind of country, a new society, a demilitarized state, a plural nation in which democracy is not only electoral but also participatory. The end of the armed conflict, however, did not mean an end to all conflicts. It did not guarantee automatic compliance with the accords and other promises that heralded the time of peace. And it did not offer a satisfactory solution to the contradictions between current economic policies and those demanded by the accords.

Five months after the historic signing, we recognized that while steps had been taken toward the desired end, new conflicts arose to challenge the credibility of the accords and the next steps in the process. In several cases, the Church's word and practice have been questioned by newspaper columnists and other players in the public sphere.

We are specifically referring to the statement of the Archdiocesan Human Rights Office, "Peace is built day by day and leads to a more perfect justice," and the grassroots pamphlet, "Christians in the face of neoliberalism"; the bulletin published by the Guatemalan Conference of Bishops, "Reflections on Land and the Current Situation in Guatemala"; the position of Bishop Alvaro Ramazzini and other bishops with respect to land invasions of private property; and the demand of the Guatemalan Conference of Religious (CONFREGUA) to end the impunity of a former military commissioner accused of committing numerous crimes in El Quiché.

The Mission to Announce the Gospel to the Poor

There is a premise, the preferential option for the poor, that will not easily be recognized as valid by those people and groups that discredit the word and work of the Church. They do not accept the Church as trying to live out Jesus' preference for the poor and needy, the millions of Guatemalans who do not have access to land, tortillas, drinking water or hospitals. They accept it even less than during the conflict. The Church adopts the point of view of the poor instead of siding unconditionally with the vision of the large landowners.

We confess that in the course of history the Church has not always been consistent with the Gospel ideal and that it still commits its share of sins today. We affirm, nevertheless, that the church authorities under attack today for defending the poor are fulfilling the prophetic role of denouncing injustice and preaching the Gospel to the poor. In some cases, those who are opposed to the action of the Church try to portray themselves as the most orthodox interpreters of biblical texts, highlighting only the spiritual meaning of the texts while rejecting any reference that does not favor the "traditional winners": established power, private property owners, those in charge of privatization. In other cases, they simply decide to use insults.

In other words, we are not returning to war but to a verbal battle between those who defend the rights of the poor and those who support the interests of the rich. It is a struggle we thought had been overcome. Are we not touching on a structural element, a cause of war, that should have been addressed in the Peace Accords? We have arrived at a conflict in which one side believes that "private property" is the Gospel, the absolute value, while for others the gospel is survival, the possibility of being able to satisfy basic needs of housing, food, health and education.

The Church would not be fulfilling its mission if we proclaimed our current situation as one of peace when there is no peace within poor families condemned to the chains of exclusion, hunger, misery, sickness and early death. We would be judged as the false prophets were judged: "They have cured the sorrow of my people by shouting peace, peace, when there was no peace" (Jeremiah 6:14). In addition, the Church would not be fulfilling its mission if it preached the Good News only in relation to the after life. Faith implies a commitment to take hold of and make real, even if only in a partial sense, the Kingdom of God, the kingdom of justice and fraternity, announced by Jesus.

Proclaiming the Gospel is incompatible with situations of injustice, exclusion and a lack of opportunities. The Gospel, on the contrary, calls on us to build a country in which all people have a place. In this sense, we understand the words of Pope John Paul II: "The Church, in virtue of its Gospel commitment, is called to be with the poor, to hear the pleas for justice and help make these a reality" (*Sollicitudo Rei Socialis,* 39:2).

We are in solidarity with the lay men and women, religious women and men, priests and bishops who are faithful to the preferential option for the poor and the Gospel, even though this faithfulness has caused them to be persecuted. We recognize in all of them an attitude like that of Jesus, which does not avoid conflicts but faces them with truth and mercy: "The Spirit of the Lord is upon me because he has anointed me; He has sent me to bring Good News to the poor" (Luke 4:18).

The Challenge of Dialogue and Reconciliation

Firm belief in the option for the poor and proclaiming the Gospel does not mean extreme or intransigent positions, which we certainly have not detected in the Church's pastoral work during the conflicts. The Church is not interested in maintaining an inflexible position that is antagonistic. On the contrary, as Christians we will never abandon our commitment to reconciliation and peace. That is why in addition to our protests of all forms of injustice and conditions that foment inequality, discrimination and exclusion—which are the roots of war—we offer our proposal to try to address all the conflicts that arise over land and private property with a sincere dialogue among all sides, with the participation of the Legal Assistance and Land Conflict Resolution Commission created through the Peace Accords.

We believe in the possibility of looking for solutions not based on particular interests. We make a call to all sides to separate ourselves as much as possible from the ideologies that so easily define our reasoning. We need to approach these meetings with the objective of learning from one another and reaching consensus, as well as being willing to hear the "cry of the land" and of those who long for bread and justice.

We call for a dialogue that does not exclude bold negotiation and solutions, that includes attention to the common good and that approaches the right of private property from a relative point of view so that the social function is not left out. Maintaining respect for the Constitution and the laws, we have to take into account the fragility of this legal situation when it comes to the asymmetrical character of land ownership in Guatemala and the need to reform it.

A World Bank study on poverty in Guatemala concluded that: "Because Guatemala needs to combine in its strategy to alleviate poverty three necessary elements—greater access by the poor to land, investment to increase the human capital of the poor, and infrastructure and support services to increase productivity—a political decision must be made by different interest groups in the country. Nevertheless, if Guatemala does not manage to maintain an adequate level of tax collection to support a successful strategy to alleviate poverty, the country can only expect lower levels of demographic growth, prolonged high poverty levels, persistent problems and growing instability" (*Guatemala: An Assessment of Poverty*, April 17, 1995).

In is also necessary to approach the bargaining table with the humility to admit that there are no easy solutions. It would not be feasible today to simply carry out a land distribution program. It would have to take into account the Mayan vision of the cosmos: Mother who gives life, center of their culture, presence of God. The specific nature of each conflict would need to be examined. It would also be important to come up with a development model for our reality that combines production for export with what is produced to meet local consumption in a way that inspires solidarity with the poorest of the poor.

There also needs to be a dialogue and transparent information on the situation of every state-owned company and diverse alternatives related to them. This does not mean being opposed to all privatization efforts, but it also does not mean that each one should be accepted without question.

We need to avoid, as a way of defending the consumer, replacing state-run monopolies with private monopolies. We need to resist the possible attempts to privatize basic state services such as education and health care, where the state's responsibility is enshrined in the Constitution. In these areas a gradual trend toward privatization is already happening. As with the case of private property, the principal issue of privatization is the common good, not just small groups motivated only by earning the highest profits in the shortest period of time.

A Church in Solidarity with the Poorest of the Poor

We do not agree with the vision that sees negotiation and dialogue as part of the past. If we want to build a strong and lasting peace we need to continue the dialogue every day. It is necessary to take on the challenge of overcoming warlike pretensions, learn to be tolerant and respectful of social, political, cultural, religious, gender and age differences, and learn to negotiate.

We reiterate our solidarity with pastoral agents and groups who make an option for the poor. They are "pacifists and builders of peace." They believe in the "foundations of law, the value of what is rational and, above all, in the transforming power of love" (*Cry for the Land*, IV, 2). In our country they represent the seeds of a Church that is called to be in solidarity with the poorest of the poor.

We repeat our call, in accordance with the peace process, to transform conflicts into opportunities for growth. Only in this way can we move towards a society that corresponds to the project of God who, as Father and Mother, wants the best for his sons and daughters. We ask God to teach us how to be just and bless our efforts for peace.

II

Option For
The Poor
In A Neoliberal
Context

The Struggle
For Survival:
Alternatives To
Neoliberalism

by Gerardo Thijssen

*When the Berlin Wall fell in 1989, and state socialism collapsed in the Soviet
Union and Eastern Europe, a new wall was erected between the North and the
South that today we call neoliberalism. In the words of Brazilian Bishop Pedro
Casaldáliga, "Neoliberalism is transnational capitalism carried to the extreme. It is the world converted into a marketplace in the service of capital
which is made into a god. Neoliberalism requires that the State be unrespon-
sive in its role as representative of the common good and the agent of public
services. Society ceases to exist, and all that is private or in the interest of
private property takes precedence. Privatization becomes the privation of life
for others, for the majority. The neoliberal doctrine is: 15 percent of humanity
has a right to live and live well; the rest is on its own."*
*One of the persons who has witnessed the impact of neoliberalism on the poor
in Mexico is Gerardo Thijssen, a Dutch priest, now laicized. After two decades
of work in Chile among the rural and urban poor, Thijssen was forced to leave
his adopted country with a brutal military coup toppled the democratically-
elected socialist government in 1973. Soon afterwards, he came to
Cuernavaca, Mexico at the invitation of Bishop Sergio Méndez Arceo.
Formerly a member of Christians for Socialism in Chile, he continues his
ministry as a lay leader of Mexico's network of base Christian communities. He
was interviewed by Jim Hodgson, a Canadian Catholic journalist, in 1997.*

We're living in a time today that is quite different from the 1960s and
1970s when I lived in Chile. It seemed then that the world was changing for
the benefit of the poor. But that has not turned out to be the case. Twenty-
five years ago, a large group of Latin American Christians, together with
Christians from North America and Europe, held the first meeting of Chris-

tians for Socialism in Chile. As Christians, we were convinced that the solution to poverty in Latin America would be found in socialism, and in Chile the people elected a socialist government before it was violently overthrown in 1973.

Socialism in the Marxist sense has not borne fruit. Our problem was that we were too European, and we based our analysis on the situation of workers in Europe. But in Latin America, there is not a large working class. Here we have an other problem to deal with: people are not only exploited, they are marginalized, too. Most people do not have salaried work, nor do they have land on which to plant crops. They live at the margins. How they survive is impressive.

I still think about socialism, but in a very different way. I think of a new society that begins from the grassroots. The alternatives that we imagined 25 years ago were very weak, very European, conceived in a different reality. Today we are thinking more from the reality in which we live. We are looking for Latin American solutions, ones which come from the people.

What is happening now in Mexico?

The situation now in Mexico is very interesting. On the one hand we have a tremendous crisis of neoliberalism. Mexico is a model of how neoliberalism functions, but it's a negative model. The consequences of exclusion, or marginalization, are very strong here. The economic crisis is strong, along with the division between rich and poor. At the same time, we see that it is among the poor that we begin to glimpse possible solutions.

This has a lot to do with the war in Chiapas. The indigenous people there want a different society. They want a different kind of politics, where the poor truly participate; where people are empowered and the task of government is to continuously inform itself about what the people want. This would be much more democratic. I think that we are advancing in terms of the meaning of democracy; we are further ahead of where we were 10 or 20 years ago.

There is a crisis of democracy in Mexico today. The people who have always held power are slowly, under pressure, opening up spaces for political opposition. In economic terms, we see thousands of small experiments to develop an alternative economy, where the goal is not just earning money, nor is it speculation, but production and distribution.

This is truly a step toward developing economic alternative, and you see it in small projects: consumer co-ops, family garden projects, production workshops, etc. People want to produce for the common good. These experiences are not well known; they don't talk on the radio and they don't write in newspapers. But the number of people involved is impressive.

We can say the same about culture. Those sectors that were considered backwards—the indigenous, women, children, elderly—are concerned about the value of human dignity, the value of women. They have a dignity that must be defended, and as social protagonists they can and do participate in creating a different kind of society.

In the base communities, we try to analyze the existing reality and understand how the character of the poor is changing. Not only do the poor feel humiliated, exploited, marginalized; they also feel they have the capacity to create something different. In terms of alternatives, we're more advanced than we were 25 years ago.

What role do the Christian base communities play in Mexico?

We continue with the Biblical reflections. For us, the word of God as it is lived is very important. We look at the present political moments, the elections, for example, or the war in Chiapas. We do workshops on neoliberalism, economic alternatives, women, peasants, alternative political platforms, etc. We no longer support, as we did in the past, revolutionary groups engaged in armed struggle—that time is past. Instead, we work closely with the civic dialogue committees. We want to dialogue, to participate peacefully as a people in the construction of a different society.

Is neoliberalism creating a situation of global apartheid?

Globalization has a positive sense. We have closer communication through e-mail, air travel and television. But this globalization coincides with a neoliberal ideology of individualism without borders, and without intervention by governments.

The problems we have in Mexico are worldwide. The gap between rich and poor is greater than ever, vast sectors of the population are marginalized, and poverty is not being eliminated. Global economies are managed by international financial institutions and transnational corporations; relatively few people control the economic system. No one else is allowed to intervene: not the Church, not the government. The market rules, and only the strongest survive. In the short term, this has brought some positive results. But the social consequences are massive.

What alternatives do you see to neoliberalism?

We Make the Road By Walking

The examples I have given of alternatives are local ones. In 1997, 2,500 delegates from the base communities gathered from all parts of Mexico. I realized then that we are all doing the same thing. We are more focused on political alternatives, looking for a true democracy, where the most important word is participation. For example, in the last state and federal elections, the PRD opposition party won several offices. The challenge we face now is how to utilize the political space that we have won. But what impresses me even more is the response of the people to globalization: the buying cooperatives, the credit unions, the workshops and nutrition programs. The solutions are very local.

What impact did the rebellion in Chiapas have on the rest of Mexico?

What began in Chiapas is now transforming itself into a national movement. It especially affected the indigenous groups, more in the south than in the north, but in the north as well. And many groups in the popular movement have finally found a group with a clear political project for the future. The relationship between the popular movements, the indigenous movements and the parties of the left is improving. The Zapatista platform has had a national impact. Solidarity is national. Things are moving forward, slowly but surely. The struggle of the people cannot be broken.

But there are still many problems. We have always seen the indigenous and the poor as objects of our help, rather than subjects of their own destiny. The Zapatistas have shown us, by the alternative that they offer, that their culture is superior to ours. In general, people believe that—in conflictive situations like central Africa, the Middle East, or Bosnia—you have to intervene militarily to maintain peace. But the Zapatistas have offered us another way: the struggle here is to convince our enemies, not vanquish them. For that reason, we negotiate and dialogue.

All this—a democratic ideal, an economy structured in favor of the people, and a different culture—gives us reason to hope: It's another way of struggling. In Chile 25 years ago, we didn't think like this. We didn't have this clarity then of the popular subject of one's destiny. This is new.

So what does the future hold?

I think neoliberalism is headed for failure. We can see that in the increasing number of marginalized people. There is no solution in sight for the problem of poverty. You look at the statistics and you can see that neoliberalism is failing. All this optimism is false; it's short-term. Perhaps a few countries will do okay, perhaps a few people will do okay, but what will they do in a world which is full of millions and millions of poor people who eventually will no longer put up with their poverty forever? There are dangers of wars and famines; all these are consequences of neoliberalism.

But we believe that there are alternatives. We see them in Mexico, perhaps on a very small scale, but alternatives nevertheless. Many people really do think differently; they want to live, produce, share, and form community. I think that the joy of forming community and being able to serve the common good is a real option and needs to be promoted, because it is already the beginning of an alternative.

Hoping Against Hope: Faith Perspectives On Women And Poverty

by Raquel Rodríguez

One of the sectors most affected by poverty is women and children. Poverty has a woman's and a children's face, and poor women and children who are indigenous or of African descent are especially vulnerable to economic policies that reduce their opportunities to the level of survival. By the same token, women have not been passive spectators or victims of injustice; they have become the protagonists of social movements that protest neoliberal policies for their impact on the poor, and they seek to create alternative models of development, at least at the local level.

Raquel Rodríguez is a Puerto Rican theologian and Disciples of Christ minister who writes frequently about women and poverty. Formerly, she worked with the Department of Ecumenical Investigations (DEI) in San José, Costa Rica. This article first appeared in PASOS, *a bimonthly journal of DEI, and was later published in the first edition of* Challenge, *EPICA's quarterly magazine at the beginning of the 1990s.*

There is no way that poverty in Latin America can be spiritualized. We would have to walk around with our eyes, ears and nose closed, in order to do so. We cannot cover it up; it is always there challenging us, questioning us. It is ugly; it cannot be idealized in either religious or human terms.

Poverty is a sin because it is an act of injustice that denies the people of Latin America the chance to live a full life. According to Gustavo Gutierrez, "Poverty is the negation of fraternity among human beings; it creates oppressive structures that benefit the few by exploiting nations, races, cultures, social classes and genders."

Poverty, then, is more than just becoming poor. The poor in Latin America are not poor of their own accord. They have been made poor. For the past five centuries, we Latin Americans have been conquered, colonized, robbed and plundered. In the words of Jon Sobrino, poverty is not "a natural phenomenon of mere scarcity, but a historical phenomenon of impoverishment."

Poverty is more than a mere economic condition. The poor not only lack material goods, but have been marginalized and alienated from the "affluent" society. This is so because they are also Black, Indian, women and children. Our governments talk a lot about having laws that protect people, that provide social services that benefit everyone, such as schools and health care. But these services never reach the poor.

Nor can the poor make themselves heard at high government levels. Only during political campaigns do the politicians outdo themselves in promises that give hope but end quickly in disillusionment. Nor do the poor have access to the "culture" that the more affluent sectors enjoy.

The condition of structural sin—injustice and oppression—does not give the poor any alternatives. It takes all their time and energy just to survive. The system is killing them.

Latin American women are marginalized by their gender, their race and their ethnic background, since a large percentage of the poor are also Indian, black, mestizo and mulatto. These additional factors make them the poorest of the poor from the biblical perspective. What could be worse, in a society that is patriarchal, hierarchical, classist and dependent, than to be a poor woman?

Poor women in Latin America incarnate the very concept of the poor that we study in the Scriptures. Their cry is rising up to God as prayer, and God listens and remembers the cries from past generations. God loves poor women because they need it the most.

The Challenge of Poverty: Death or the Fullness of Life

Poverty challenges women. They can either accept their lot with resignation—accept a life of dying—or fight for a decent life. The struggle is not just on their own behalf. It is also a struggle for the lives of their children. Women have accepted this challenge and are becoming authors of their own history.

They do so not because they necessarily understand their oppression and marginalization as women but simply because they love life. They engender and give birth to life. They fight for life. First of all, these women erupt into history as mothers, the traditional role society has assigned to them. Then, they leave the home for the workplace; and from there they begin organizing as women for better conditions. In doing so, awareness of gender oppression emerges.

We Make the Road By Walking

As part of this process, Latin American women are developing two new related concepts. First, they realize that there is no way to achieve real justice for the poor, particularly marginalized women, under the present system. There has to be a drastic social transformation if everyone is to live a full and dignified life. Secondly, women are developing a deep sense of solidarity with each other. They are not fighting only for their own lives or for their loved ones, but for the lives of their neighbors and their neighbors' children, and the lives of future generations.

Women are not the only ones involved in this process. They are immersed in the struggle alongside the marginalized men of Latin America. The poor of both sexes are coming together to fight against injustice. The difference is that women are also aware of the special oppression they suffer because of their gender. Carmen Lora writes, "The woman who demands a better life does not do so to put down men but in order to obtain better conditions for all human beings. From that point she begins to look critically at her relationships with both sexes."

The experience of Nicaraguan women has been one of the most encouraging examples of this process. Oppression under the Somoza regime led women to abandon their homes and traditional roles and join organizations confronting the system that was pushing them towards death. They joined the insurrection because they were poor and exploited, not because they felt oppressed as women. In the process, however, they opened their eyes and demanded justice, not only as poor people but also as women who were doubly oppressed. They helped transform their society and continue the struggle. They helped bring forth a new concept of solidarity among women and learned the meaning of giving up one's life so that others might live.

Latin American Women and Their New Concept of God

Within the liberation process, women have discovered a new concept of God. They have come to understand that they are not only witnesses to the Good News but also that the Gospel was intended for them. They have discovered that God is not neutral, that God chooses to love particularly the poor, the oppressed and those marginalized by society. Further, poor women have found that the God of the Exodus listens to the cries of the oppressed and helps them overcome their oppression. They have discovered that as in the Beatitudes, the God of love announces the end of their suffering and calls them "the blessed ones," "the lucky ones," "the favored ones" and "the fortunate ones."

Poor women don't fear God but rather count on God for comfort, strength and understanding. They have developed a new relationship with God on the basis of being part of the *"anawim,"* the poor of Yahweh, in both the historical and religious sense. These women are those who have nothing more to lose, and therefore can give themselves fully to God's immeasurable love without reservation. They are like the widow in the Temple who gave the little she had without worrying about her next meal. They are women who can give all they have left—their lives—without worrying, just hoping for a better future.

New Spirituality, New Strength

These women have also discovered a new Jesus, the Jesus of the Good News. It is the Jesus who preached about abundant life, the one who came to transform an unjust and oppressive system and restore dignity to women. Rediscovering Jesus and his call to life has given Latin American women a renewed strength and hope in the midst of adversity.

This is a whole new dimension of spirituality and one vital to the liberation process. In the struggle for life, hope prevails over death and suffering. There is joy and celebration because the poor women of Latin America look to a different future that those in rich countries and oppressors in our countries will never understand. It is "the stubborn presence of joy" in the midst of pain, suffering, oppression and death.

Hope for the future arises out of the desperation of death, like a rising phoenix. Suffering causes pain but not despair, so that there is always time for celebration. We celebrate the little things, those things that signal an end to the battle and the final victory of life over death. A Latin American woman writes: "Joy is born from faith, from the hope that death is not the last word. That is why we can already celebrate, at this very moment. In the midst of the war, we find the joy of the resurrection."

One thing which gives great meaning to poor women is the rediscovery of the death and resurrection of Jesus. They have begun to understand his death as an act of self-giving for the lives of the weakest ones. His crucifixion is a consequence of his ministry, his teachings, his actions for justice, so that the poor and oppressed gain access to a fuller life.

Women understand his resurrection as a triumph of life over death and oppression, the triumph of justice over injustice in anticipation of that final victory: the new creation of God. This new way of conceiving the death and resurrection of Jesus is quite different from that which is often preached, for it allows women to keep on fighting for the liberation process even when surrounded by death. This new vision enables women to celebrate the deaths of those who have fallen in the cause of life and to see the martyrs resurrected in the lives of the others who continue the good fight.

These daring women have called to us as Christians to side with them, just as Jesus and God have done, and to read the Bible from their perspective. Latin American women not only identify with women in the Bible but also with the whole message of life, hope and Good News that the Scriptures offer us. Their experience helps us to understand certain passages that are not very clear when interpreted from a traditional perspective.

Mary: A New Symbol for Women

The angel said to her, "Mary, do not be afraid. Your are to conceive and bear a son and you must name him Jesus." Mary said to the angel, "But how can this come about, since I am a virgin?" (Luke 1:30,34)

By rediscovering liberation in the Bible, women have rediscovered Mary. Their discovery has been crucial for all of us. Our people are mainly Catholics. The figure of Mary forms an important part of the Catholic tradition, but one that has been used to keep women submissive. Mary is portrayed as "humble" in the submissive sense, that is, as someone who would not talk back; who accepted without questioning and kept her emotions hidden. Mary is the suffering mother who stoically accepted her punishment, including the death of her own son, without uttering a protest.

Poor women, who grew up within this belief system, have rejected the tradition and discovered another Mary. This Mary asked questions before accepting her role as an instrument for God's incarnation of the Messiah. She knew how to think and wanted to know what was sought of her, what was God's purpose. What would be the consequences of her decision to bear the Messiah or to refuse? As a poor person, she shared in the suffering of her people. She knew that unjust social structures must be transformed, and so Mary accepted God's call in the only way society would allow: as a mother. She bore the child and knowingly gave him up for the lives of others.

Isn't this the same thing that is happening to so many women in Latin America today? They have entered into the liberation process as mothers and many of them have given their beloved sons and daughters for the lives of others. They too should be called "blessed" by future generations.

Hagar: Mother of Nations

And Sarah said to Abraham, "May the wrong done to me be on you. I gave my maid Hagar to your embrace and when she saw that she conceived she looked down on me in contempt." She said to Abraham, "Get this slave woman out with her son!" But God said to Abraham, "I will make a nation of the son of the slave woman" (Genesis 16:5, 21:10, 13).

In telling the history of salvation, we often forgot the story of Hagar and Ishmael. We remember only the story of Abraham and Sarah who, with their descendants, were blessed by the promise that a great nation would be born from them (Genesis 11). But for poor women of today, Sarah represents the traditional upper-class "mistress of the house." Latin American women, especially those of Central America, have discovered Hagar and Ishmael, too. Hagar, by contrast, is a poor woman who has to work as a servant to feed her children. Like many women today, she has no choice but to put up with the whims of her mistress and comply with the sexual demands of the master or risk losing her job.

Women can identify with Hagar's suffering when she is thrown out of the house because she is pregnant with the employer's child. They can identify with Hagar's iron will to struggle for her life and for that of her son Ishmael. Hagar incarnates the life and willpower of many unwed mothers, abandoned women or widows whose husbands have been politically assassinated. These women have had to struggle alone to raise their children and to run the household, all of this within a patriarchal culture.

Hagar was a servant when she was thrown out of Abraham and Sarah's household and yet she was blessed by God. God's blessing is a sign of hope and celebration poor women can never forget. These women understand why, because of Hagar, the course of salvation history is more complicated, because they themselves are complicating the course of history in Latin America today.

I have come to believe that no woman will ever forget God's affirmation of the poor. Even though God is the God of Abraham, Isaac and Jacob, God is also the God Hagar and Ishmael. God blessed them too, and promised to make from Hagar's son, Ishmael, a great nation. This promise of liberation will be realized in future generations precisely because poor Latin American women embody that promise.

For Life
And Against
Neoliberalism:
Jesuits Speak Out

from a Statement by the Jesuits of Latin America

One of the strongest statements to critique neoliberalism is a letter of the Jesuit provincials of Latin America to their friends. In 1996, the Jesuits of Latin America met in Mexico to draw up a letter and a working document in which they denounced the neoliberal ideology and economy with lucidity and conviction. In it they conclude: "Men and women will always be threatened by greed for wealth, ambition for power and the insatiable search for sensory satisfactions. Today this threat is made concrete in neoliberalism, and tomorrow it will have other ideological expressions and there will be other idols. We have been called in the Church to contribute to the liberation of our brothers and sisters from human disorder and we will remain there, in this task at the service of all, placing ourselves on the side of our friends the poor, because that is what our Lord Jesus did." The following declaration was published in the February-March 1997 edition of Envío Magazine, *a publication of the Central American University (UCA) in Managua, Nicaragua.*

Dear friends,

We Provincial Superiors of the Society of Jesus in Latin America and the Caribbean, following the call of General Congregation 34 to deepen our faith-justice mission, want to share some reflections on the so-called neoliberalism in our countries with all of those who are participating in this apostolic mission of the Society of Jesus throughout the continent, and with all who are concerned about and committed to the destiny of our people, especially the poorest.

We refuse to calmly accept that the economic measures applied in recent years in all Latin American countries and the Caribbean are the only possible way to orient the economy, and that the impoverishment of millions of Latin Americans is the inevitable cost of future growth. Behind these economic measures lies a strategic policy, an underlying concept of the human being and culture that must be discerned from the perspective of the models of society we aspire to and work for, at the side of so many men and women moved by the hope of life and of leaving future generations a more just and human society.

The considerations presented do not pretend to be a scientific analysis of a complex issue that requires research from the point of view of many disciplines. They are only reflections that we find pertinent on the consequences and criteria of neoliberalism; and characteristics of the society that we desire. Our primary concern in sharing these reflections is religious and ethical. The political and economic behavior we refer to reflects in the public terrain the limits and countervalues of a culture based on a concept of the individual and of human society that is far from the Christian ideal.

The Society of Which We Are a Part

On the threshold of the 21st century, communications link us closely together, technology gives us new possibilities of knowledge and creativity, and the market penetrates all social spaces. In contrast to the past decade, the economy of the majority of our countries has once again begun to grow.

This material boom, which could create hope for all, actually leaves multitudes in poverty, with no chance of participating in the construction of a common destiny. It threatens cultural identity and destroys natural resources. We calculate that at least 180 million people live in poverty in Latin America and the Caribbean and 80 million live in extreme poverty.

The economic dynamics that produce these perverse effects tend to transform into ideologies and to make certain concepts absolute: the market, for example, goes from being a useful and even necessary instrument to increase and improve supply and reduce prices to being the means, the method and the end governing relations between human beings.

To achieve this, measures known as neoliberal have been generalized throughout the continent. These measures:

- put economic growth, rather than the full harmony of men and women with creation, as the economy's raison d'etre;
- restrict state intervention by taking away any state responsibility for the minimum goods that every citizen deserves as a human being;
- eliminate general programs that create opportunities for all, replacing them with occasional support to focal groups;
- privatize businesses according to the argument that the state is always a bad administrator;

• open the borders to merchandise, capital and financial flow without restriction, leaving the smallest and weakest producers without sufficient protection;

• remain silent about the foreign debt problem, the payment of which necessitates drastic cuts in social spending;

• subordinate the complexity of public finances to macroeconomic variables: a balanced fiscal budget, reduced inflation and stable balance of payments, as if the common good follows from that and does not generate new problems for the population that must be attended to;

• insist that the adjustments will produce growth that, once voluminous, will raise income levels and resolve the situation of the less favored;

• motivate private investment by eliminating obstacles that protective labor legislation could impose;

• exonerate powerful groups from paying taxes and from environmental obligations, protecting them so as to accelerate the industrialization process, thereby provoking an even greater concentration of wealth and economic power;

• put political activity at the service of this economic policy, leading to the paradox of eliminating all barriers to the free market while at the same time placing social and political controls—for example on the free contracting of labor—to guarantee the hegemony of the free market.

We must recognize that these adjustment measures have also had positive results. It is enough to mention the contribution of market mechanisms to increasing the supply of better-quality goods at lower prices; the drop in inflation all over the continent; the removal from government of tasks that do not pertain to them so they can dedicate themselves, if they choose, to the common good; the general consciousness of fiscal austerity that uses public resources better; and the advance in trade relations among our nations.

But these elements hardly compensate for the immense imbalances and perturbations neoliberalism causes through the concentration of income, wealth and land ownership; the multiplication of the unemployed urban masses or those surviving in unstable and unproductive jobs; the bankruptcy of thousands of small- and medium-sized businesses; the destruction and forced displacement of indigenous and peasant populations; the expansion of drug trafficking based in rural sectors whose traditional products can no longer compete; the disappearance of food security; an increase in criminality often triggered by hunger; the destabilization of national economies by the free flow of international speculation; and maladjustments in local communities by multinational companies that do not take the residents into account.

As a consequence, together with moderate economic growth, social unrest expressed in citizen protests and strikes is increasing in almost all of our countries. Armed struggle, which resolves nothing, is emerging again in some areas. There is increased rejection of the general economic orientation that, far from improving the common good, deepens the traditional causes of popular discontent: inequality, poverty and corruption.

The Concept of the Human Being

Behind the economic rationality that calls itself neoliberal is a concept of the human being that reduces the greatness of men and women to their ability to generate monetary income. It exacerbates individualism and the desire to earn and possess, and easily moves to an attack on the integrity of creation. In many cases it unleashes greed, corruption and violence. When it is generalized among social groups, it radically destroys the community.

Thus is imposed an order of values that stresses the individual liberty to seek the consumption of satisfaction and pleasures; that legitimizes, among other things, drugs and eroticism without restrictions. Such a freedom rejects any state interference in private initiative, opposes social planning, rejects the virtue of solidarity and accepts only the laws of the market.

Through the economic globalization process, this way of understanding men and women penetrates our countries with symbolic content that is very seductive. Thanks to the domination of the mass media, it breaks the roots of local cultural identities that powerless to communicate their message.

Our society's leaders, linked into these globalizing movements and indiscriminately accepting the market forces, commonly live as foreigners in their own countries. Without dialoguing with the people, they consider the people an obstacle and danger to their own interests, rather than brothers and sisters, partners or friends.

In a more general way, this concept considers it normal for millions of men and women to be born and die in abject poverty all over the continent, unable to generate the income to buy a more human quality of life. Governments and societies are not scandalized by the hunger and uncertainty of the multitudes who are made desperate and perplexed by the excesses of those who use the resources of society and nature without thinking about others.

The Society We Seek

Thank God, there are transformation initiatives that insinuate the rise of a new world from diverse cultural, ethnic, generational, gender and social sectors. Animated by these efforts, we want to help build a reality closer to the Gospel's kingdom of justice, solidarity and fraternity, where life with dignity is possible for all men and women.

We seek a society where every person has access to the goods and services that he or she deserves for having been called to share this common walk to God. We are not demanding a welfare society, one of unlimited material satisfactions, but a just society, where no one is excluded from work or from access to fundamental goods for personal development such as education, nutrition, health care, housing, and security.

We seek a society where we can all live as a family and look to the future with hope, sharing nature and leaving its marvels for future generations to enjoy. A society attentive to the cultural traditions that gave identity to indigenous peoples, to those who came from other places, to African Americans and to mixed peoples. A society aware of the weak, the marginalized, those who have suffered the impact of socioeconomic processes that do not put human beings first. A democratic society, built with participation, where political activity is the option of those who want to dedicate themselves to the service of everyone's general interests.

We are aware that achieving this kind of society has a high price because it demands changes in attitude, habits and values. We are challenged to make the positive elements of modernity our own, such as work, organization and efficiency, without which we could not build that society of which we dream. Finally, we want to contribute to building a Latin American community among our people.

The Tasks Before Us

We have before us an enormous task to be carried out in different fields:

• To undertake an intellectual effort of great importance in the social sciences, theology and philosophy to study neoliberalism, working alongside many others in our universities and our study, research and promotion centers to explain its deepest rationality, and the effects it has on human beings and nature; and
• To discern and weigh the lines of action that emerge from this analysis, choosing pertinent options.

This knowledge and these decisions should lead us to:

• Accompany the victims from communities of solidarity, protecting the rights of the excluded and undertaking with them, in dialogue with decision-making sectors, to build the most inclusive society possible.

• Strengthen our people's cultural and spiritual traditions so that they can situate themselves in the global community, from their own identity, without diminishing their symbolic richness and community spirit.

• Incorporate into our educational work the kinds of values necessary to form people able to preserve the primacy of human beings in the world we share.

• Give students the necessary preparation to understand and work to transform that reality.

• Resist particularly the consumer society and its ideology of happiness based on unlimited buying of material satisfactions.

• Communicate through every means the results of the analysis of neoliberalism, the values that should be preserved and promoted, and possible alternatives.

• Propose viable solutions in places where global and macroeconomic decisions are made.

We will work to strengthen the value of gratuity, in a world where everything is bought for a price; to stimulate the sense of a sober life and simple beauty; to favor the interior silence and spiritual quest; and to invigorate a responsible use of freedom, integrating a sense of solidarity from the spirituality of Saint Ignatius of Loyola with a decided commitment to the transformation of the human heart.

To make our pledge believable, to demonstrate our solidarity with the excluded of the continent, and to show our distance from consumerism, we will commit ourselves not only to personal austerity, but to ensuring that our works and institutions avoid all types of ostentation, using means coherent with our poverty. Our investment and consumption policies will not support businesses that notoriously infringe on human rights and damage the ecology. In this way we want to reaffirm the radical option of faith that led us to respond to God's call to follow Jesus in poverty, to be more effective and free in the search for justice.

We will seek with many others a national and Latin American community of solidarity, where science, technology, and the markets are at the service of all members of our peoples. Where the commitment to the poor makes evident that working for the plenitude of all men and women, without exclusion, is our contribution, modest and serious, to the greater glory of God in history and in creation.

We hope that these reflections animate the efforts to improve our service to the Latin American people. We ask our Lady of Guadalupe, Patroness of Latin America, to bless our people and to intercede so that we may obtain abundant grace to carry out our mission.

Christian Base Communities Confront The Neoliberal Project

by Juan Manuel Hurtado

Neoliberalism and its impact on the poor in Latin America has been critiqued by social scientists, economists and theologians and the poor. At a 1997 meeting of Latin American Christians in Sao Paolo, Brazil, a workshop was held called "Christians in search of an alternative to neoliberalism." The final declaration concluded: "Our criticism of neoliberalism is radical, and based on Gospel values. Neoliberalism is a project built on the basis of a global society under the hegemony of capital and presented as the only rational way to organize society. Neoliberalism does not comply with the function of the economy that offers all human beings the basic goods to satisfy material and cultural needs; on the contrary, it means the death of millions of people." In the following declaration, Juan Manuel Hurtado offers the perspective of the Christian Base Communities of Mexico. This article appeared in the July 1992 edition of Estudios Ecuménicos.

After the fall of the socialist bloc and its opening to the market economy, it would appear that the only valid economic and political model of society left to the world is capitalism. Neoliberalism (the present model of capitalism) grows stronger every day and allows the powerful to accumulate more wealth and power; it also generates hunger, misery, underdevelopment and death in Third World countries.

The law of the market, of competition, is the law of the survival of the fittest. Wealthy corporations and technologically powerful nations join together to destroy their "enemies," basing their actions on economic, political and even theological logic. From this perspective we may analyze the US invasion of Panama, the Gulf war, the economic and political blockade of the Sandinista government in Nicaragua, and the current blockade of Cuba.

This is the absolute law of the Empire that excludes anyone outside of its reign, the law of the jungle that is directly opposed to any democratic aspiration or struggle for human rights. And as somebody has already warned: "If the law of the jungle rules, we are not the lion."

The number of poor people and the level of poverty is increasing throughout the world. In Latin America, governments impose economic measures on the poor in accordance with the requirements of the IMF (International Monetary Fund) and giant multinational corporations rather than responding to the needs of the impoverished majority. A good example of this subservience to rich corporations is Mexico's rush to establish the North American Free Trade Agreement (NAFTA) with the United States and Canada.

Our cultures and our way of life have been inundated by consumer products promoted by the multinational corporations, which canonize technology and consumerism as the only model of society. This violates the cultural rights of our peoples, particularly those of indigenous or African descent, and the ways we express ourselves. If in the past gold was traded for glass beads, today quality resources are traded for alcohol and Coca-Cola.

A People in Resistance

The failure of peoples of indigenous and African descent, farm workers and marginalized peoples in the cities to assimilate into the great neoliberal project is characterized by governments today as nonconformity, backwardness, noncompliance with the economic and political strategies of the nation, lack of understanding of the current economic model or separation from the "national project."

The legitimate organization of the people to defend their interests is seen as protest. The poor are only taken into account when their culture and their creativity become objects of consumption, when their hospitality and solidarity are noted, or when their cheap and docile labor is required.

When the poor take responsibility for their own lives, when they want to create their own social and economic project in accordance with their past, their interests and their possibilities, then the governments, the multinational corporations and the establishment press attack them. Our peoples are resisting, and struggling to survive and to move forward.

Over the years the poor have responded to the assault of capitalism with suffering and with organization. They have known how to conserve the miracle of life. With ingenuity they have multiplied their bread to feed their children and unmask the death-dealing policies of the powerful for what they truly are. The 43,000 people who die of hunger each day in the world are both evidence of and an accusation against the evil of this project of death.

Christian Base Communities and the Life of the Poor

But neoliberalism is not the only model of society; there is an alternative. The experience of the Christian base communities provides a model whose primary focus is the life of the poor. Throughout Latin America and the Third World, Christian base communities have appeared as a new and authentic expression of Church and society which is more communitarian, more committed to service and more rooted in the lives of the people.

Here the poor have found a place to express the rich potential of their culture and their longing for liberation; here too the Gospel has taken root in the history of our peoples. Because the Christian base communities are rooted in the daily struggle of the poor to live, and because the majority of the leaders are lay people, the communities provide an example of a Christianity which offers an alternative way of life and hope to the poor.

Against the flood of neoliberal policies that subjugate our people, another current flows quietly and unnoticed: the voice and the life of the poor. This current cannot be mistaken for the flood; its waters flow from another source. What are some of the characteristics of this current?

The People's Project of Life

The people who live in the Christian base communities possess another logic of life, another language, another symbolism that goes beyond the society of supply and demand, beyond "the god of free enterprise" to which our governments, devoid of any moral stature, have rendered homage.

What matters is the memory of our martyrs and the radical values of Christianity. Sharing and solidarity, prophetic denunciation and silent witness are fundamental examples of the culture of life of the Christian base communities. All this creates a rich symbolism of life, rooted in the immense creativity and joy of our people and their struggle for a fraternal society.

The logic of the Christian base communities is the logic of hope, the language is the language of bearing witness, and the utopia is the utopia of the dawning of a new society. To return to our roots is to move forward towards a future when people are reconciled with each other.

The new society is born at the base. It is in community that the model of a new society is being constructed; it is in community where the values of a new society—mutual respect, equality, democracy, freedom—can be lived. In this sense the Christian base communities present a model and a precursor of life in a new society.

III

The Indigenous
Face
Of The
Church

This Ground
Is Holy:
The Guatemalan
Highlands

by Fernando Bermúdez

For a long time the suffering of Guatemala has been hidden from view. During the 1980s, indigenous peasants organized to defend their rights to land and to just working conditions in the seasonal harvests of coffee and cotton. Many supported the liberation movement of the URNG guerrillas when no other option was available to them to vindicate their rights. Consequently, the military carried out a scorched-earth campaign in indigenous regions of Guatemala, massacring tens of thousands. Many indigenous peasants fled to the refugee camps in southern Mexico; thousands more remained in Guatemala, many of them organizing themselves in the Communities of Population in Resistance (CPRs) in the mountains of El Quiché and El Peten.
In the following reflection, Fernando Bermúdez narrates his journey to the Sierra highlands, and portrays the indigenous face of the Guatemalan Church. He is a Catholic priest working with the formation of catechists and Christian base communities, and he is on the editorial team of the magazine Voces. *He is also the author of* Death and Resurrection in Guatemala *(ORBIS, 1985).*

On February 15-25, 1993, for the first time in their 12 years of existence, a visit by land was made to the Communities of Population in Resistance (CPRs) in Quiché. The caravan was made up of Catholic bishops and Evangelical pastors, labor union leaders and members of popular organizations, journalists and visitors from 14 other countries.

The mission began with the celebration of the Eucharist in the cathedral, presided over by Bishop Julio Cabrera, from Quiché: "Wash your feet, because the land where you are going is holy land, watered with the blood of countless martyrs. You are going to meet crucified Christs from the Communities of Population in Resistance, to see them with your own eyes, to hear them and to touch them. You are going to help them come down from the cross and offer your solidarity to them. Pay attention to them, they have much to teach us. They have been formed in the school of suffering."

Following the Star of Hope

The caravan left Guatemala City on February 15, with 200 people going to the CPRs in the Sierra highlands and 200 going to the CPRs in the Ixcán jungle. I joined the caravan to the Sierra highlands. In each of the towns where we stopped along the way we were offered food and shelter. Fireworks and the music of the Mayan flute and drum greeted us, and signs were strung across the church towers that read: "Blessed are the peacemakers!"

In the town of Nebaj, the parish priest read the Gospel story of the Three Kings who came to pay homage to Jesus, born in a poor manger. We too had seen a star, a sign of God in the midst of the Guatemalan people. We were walking to greet the poor and humble Jesus who lives in the communities of resistance, hidden in the mountains of Quiché.

The Herods of today, like those of yesterday, do not recognize Jesus' presence there. They only know how to command their armies to massacre the innocent children of Bethlehem, the innocent children today who represent hope for a new life, distinct from the old and corrupt society.

It was night by the time we arrived in the town of Chajul. The enemies of peace had cut off the electricity in the town. Despite threats from the leaders of the civil defense patrols, people came out to greet us, holding candles in their hands and singing songs and chants. The parish priest cried out:

"People are tired of the war. They want peace. Let us begin to build peace by extending our hands to our brothers and sisters in the communities of resistance. We want to visit them with open hearts. We must not listen to those who only stir up division in our town and oppose the CPRs."

The following day we traveled by bus to the village of Juil; from this point on we traveled on foot. As we walked, we came across two crosses, one which read "Father José Maria Grán" and the other "Domingo Batz." Father José and Domingo were a parish priest and a catechist from the parish of Chajul who were assassinated at this spot by the military on June 4, 1980. Truly we are in a land of martyrs, standing on holy ground that has been profaned by the powers of death.

We began to climb the steep ridges of the majestic Cuchumatán Mountains which reach up to the clouds, the tropical vegetation covering the slopes given to landslides. When we reached the village of Vichox, near the summit of the mountain, more than a hundred men and women from the communities of resistance were there to greet us and accompany us on the rest of the journey to the CPRs.

"We hope that your visit will help us break the military encirclement of our communities," they told us. It was our first encounter with people from the communities of resistance.

For the next two hours we celebrated a fiesta, complete with greetings, fireworks, chants and songs. From this vantage point we could see the ridge on the other side of the Xalbal River, and numerous "model villages" built by the army as a way to control the civilian population. These beautiful mountains have been the site of cruel bombings, terror and bloodshed in the 1980s, when more than 450 villages were burned to the ground under the military "scorched earth" campaign.

Later that morning we walked down to the river, and climbed up the path which winds its way along another steep ridge, only a few feet from a precipitous vertical drop. We passed La Perla, a plantation whose owner, "the Tiger of Ixcán," terrorized the indigenous population until he was killed by the guerrillas in 1976. Along the way several Ixil women, in their multi-colored garb, joined us, walking barefoot as they had done for centuries over timeless paths that seemed to lead toward the Third Millennium.

A Night in the "Model Village" of Chel

After ten hours of a strenuous hike, we passed through the idyllic village of Jua before reaching the "model village" of Chel, the army's point of departure for its attacks against the communities of resistance, and our destination for the night. The heavily-armed civil defense patrol exercises strict control over everyone who enters or leaves the village. They greeted us with a burst of machine-gun fire into the air, hoping to terrorize us.

Ninety-six people were massacred in Chel at the beginning of the 1980s. Among those massacred were many children whose bodies were smashed against the rocks and then thrown into the river. The survivors of this massacre were forced to flee by night and to take refuge in the mountains.

Afterward the army build this "model village." It is nothing more than a concentration camp, populated by people hiding in the mountains who were later captured by the army.

Some people in the village of Chel told us that the head of the civil defense patrol told them not to offer us food or shelter. The civil patrols openly oppose the communities of resistance. Representatives of the CPRs who accompanied our caravan spoke to the people in the village, telling them that the people of the CPRs are their relatives. They reached out to the people of Chel and asked them not to obey the orders of the civil patrols and the army.

We gathered in the center of the village to celebrate our arrival, with music and greetings. Many people listened from the doors of their houses, but they did not venture to come out. The charismatics and evangelicals, on the other hand, organized a religious service to disrupt our gathering. They put loudspeakers at full volume, and sang until late into the night. We were exhausted from our journey, hungry and thirsty, and they didn't even offer us a glass of water.

Early the next morning we continued our journey through the mountains. Leaving rivers and valleys behind, we began to climb the narrow, muddy, zigzagging path to the summit. As we walked, we penetrated deeper and deeper into the dense forest vegetation of the mountain. Every now and then the call of a *zaraguate* bird reminded us that we were in a forest. The sun shone above us through the tops of the tall trees; a deep green darkness surrounded us below as we passed beside an occasional stream flowing between the rocks and shrubs.

Encounter with the CPRs

We were just an hour from the communities of resistance when we were greeted along the path by men and women from the CPRs. They offered us coffee from large clay pots, as well as tortillas and malanga. I recalled the verse from a song that says: "When the poor, who have nothing, share; when the weak offer encouragement, God is present in our midst." A Quiché woman, as soon as she saw the CPR villages in the distance, knelt down and kissed the earth.

We entered the region of Cabá, our destination. People had been waiting hours just to greet us and offer us hospitality in their humble houses made of bamboo walls and thatched roofs. I stayed with a young indigenous couple and their five children. I had never seen such a poor house. They had nothing in their house, yet we always seemed to have enough to eat.

The houses in the communities of resistance don't have doors; they don't need them. There is a high degree of morality. Everyone, men or women, young or old, can walk alone at day or at night and know they will be safe. There is no delinquency here. Everyone respects everyone else, and they live together as brothers and sisters. Their only fear is the invasions by the army and the civil defense patrols that sometimes result in people being captured or assassinated, and possessions being destroyed.

At the beginning of the 1980s, there were more than 60,000 people living in the communities of resistance; now there are only 30,000, due to the repression. Many were killed by the army, many died of hunger, and many were captured. The people live in dozens of CPR villages in three different regions of the Sierra highlands: Cabá, Santa Clara and Xeputúl.

There is poverty in the Communities of Population in Resistance in the Sierra mountains. Many people have gone for years wearing the same clothes, and some people cover themselves with leaves from trees or pieces of plastic. For years the army came and killed their domestic animals and burned their crops; for the last two years, however, no one has gone hungry. Everybody feels part of the same family.

Building a New Society In the Ruins of the Old

Traditionally, indigenous people in the Guatemalan highlands migrated to the southern coast five or six months of the year to harvest coffee, sugarcane or cotton. Now it's no longer necessary. People in the CPRs can sustain their families from what they themselves produce, mainly corn and beans. They work five days a week for the community, and two days a week for their own families. There are no salaries, and very little money.

"We have proved to ourselves," Marcelino, one of the catechists, told me, "that if we work together we can produce the crops we need to survive for the entire year. We don't pay taxes, nor rent the land. We've found that all of us, by our work, can contribute to developing the community, whether it is in production, education, health care or pastoral work. Education and health care are both free."

The educational system that they have developed is called "Education for the New Society." The teachers are men and women who have had some schooling. Besides teaching the children to read and write, they try to help them learn about and exercise their basic rights. They practice democracy, and carry out some responsibilities in the community. They study Guatemalan history from a critical perspective, listen to the news on the radio, and even make a simple analysis of the national and international situation.

The children go to school on Monday, Wednesday and Friday. On the other days they work in the fields or perform other community tasks. There are twenty schools in the communities of resistance in the Sierra highlands, all built with stick walls and straw roofs. Before the children had pencils and notebooks, they used pieces of charcoal and wooden slates.

Despite these hardships, the people have achieved a remarkable degree of organization and human development. They have formed agricultural cooperatives, health and education committees, women's groups, development projects, and religious services for Catholics, Evangelicals and those who practice the traditional Mayan religion.

Everyone contributes to the community according to his or her capacity, and each one receives according to his or her needs. I was struck by the joy and happiness that is reflected in the faces of the people, and their great capacity for hospitality. They enjoyed sharing what little they have with us.

Formed in the School of Suffering

On the first day of our three-day visit to the communities of resistance, we met in the center of a field in Cabá. Different members of the coordinating commission of the CPRs in the Sierra highlands spoke to us about their history: "Our resistance is rooted in the last 500 years. But it was only 12 years ago that we began to demand our rights, and the army began to capture, torture, massacre and destroy our villages. It's because of this repression that we had to take refuge in these mountains to save our lives.

"We have suffered hunger, cold, rain and bombings in these mountains. We have nourished ourselves on roots and herbs. Many of our brothers and sisters got sick and many others died of hunger. Others were captured, tortured and killed. Others were imprisoned in 'model villages.' The army keeps an eye on us so that we cannot plant; and the soldiers destroy our crops so that we will die of hunger.

"All this suffering taught us to organize in order to survive. We grow corn, beans, malanga, plantains, pineapple and coffee. Each family cultivates what it needs to feed itself. The land belongs to the community. In the assembly we decide who is going to cultivate which plot. Some lands are communal lands that are worked collectively, on a rotating basis, so that we can support the work of the teachers and health promoters, and help the widows, orphans and the sick.

"The civil defense patrol in Chel says these lands do not belong to us, because we haven't paid for them. But we say they have been paid for, not with money but with our blood."

The indigenous peasants in the CPRs speak of the land as something sacred, as though speaking of their own mother. When an indigenous peasant opens a furrow to plant corn, he or she asks pardon of "mother earth" for injuring her. "Mother earth" is the one who gives the people food, who gives them life, who offers them security, and who receives them when they die. That's why the peasant identifies with the land and loves it. A peasant without land is like a person without a soul.

For the indigenous peasant, the landowners are usurpers who steal from the "mother earth" because God created the land for everyone. The land cannot be bought or sold, just as no one would buy or sell his own mother. That's how one understands the struggle of peasants for land. It is a sacred struggle. It is a just struggle.

The Blood of the Martyrs

Before we left to return to Guatemala City, we celebrated a memorial for the martyrs. There is not a single family that does not have three or more martyrs. One person told us: "The martyrs are not just a memory. They live in the heart of our people. All this blood, all these lives torn from the earth, we feel present with us; they are examples that strengthen us. They preferred to die rather than stain themselves with the blood of their people."

We all gathered in the soccer field where the memorial celebration of the martyrs was taking place. Each family carried its own cross, with the names of the family members who were martyred, their ages, and the manner in which they were killed: some were shot, others burned alive, others died in bombing raids, others were tortured to death. Some of the crosses had 12 names on them.

The procession brought tears to the eyes of the visitors. I felt that God was present there with us, at the side of the poor, of the crucified ones, vindicating them, and resurrecting them to a new life of peace, justice and love. We continued the procession, singing: "You are crucified on the cross, massacred by the powerful ones. Today you offer your blood again in the blood or our martyrs. Hear us, O Lord, hear the cry of your people."

We climbed a hill, the hill of the martyrs, and deposited our crosses there. Then we celebrated an ecumenical service, marked by signs of hope and life: "Our brothers and sisters have died for the Kingdom of God, which is greater than all the armies combined. We are the remnant of the blood of the martyrs. We give you thanks because our martyrs live in the resistance."

A New Model of Church

A new model of church is emerging in the CPRs, in which lay people actively participate in its ministries and mission. A liberating and prophetic church committed to peace and justice, unattached to power and wealth. A church that defends life and serves the people. An ecumenical church, open to dialogue with evangelicals, Mayan religion and nonbelievers. A church of the poor, born of the suffering and the blood of the martyrs.

One catechist, Marcelino, shared these thoughts with us: "We have lived the passion of Jesus. We have been born again with new life in our communities. Our faith in Christ is our strength. We say with St. Paul: 'Who can

91

separate us from the love of Christ? Tribulation? Anguish? Persecution? Hunger? Lack of clothing? Danger? The sword? In everything we are victorious thanks to the One who loved us' (Romans 8:35-37).

"We have suffered together here, together we have protected ourselves. Neither persecution, nor bombs, nor hunger, nor cold, nor fear have divided us; instead we have united even more as brothers and sisters."

The CPRs, with all of their limitations, are a seed of hope, not only for Guatemala but for the entire world. They offer an alternative model of society to the consumer, competitive and violent society in which we live.

Their new, simple, communitarian and peaceful way of life—and communion with the mountains, the land, the water, the wind, the sun, the animals—contrasts with the reality of the other Guatemala of injustice, exploitation, competition, individualism, hunger, illiteracy, theft, murder and rape.

We lived a time of *kairos* in the CPRs, a time of grace. Now I can say with conviction that the Christian utopia is possible in our land. Our brothers and sisters in the communities of resistance teach us that it is possible to live a new way of life, different than the neoliberal capitalist system that arrogantly presents itself as the only the definitive alternative in history.

In the CPRs I saw for myself that it is possible to live the ideal of the first Christians, and the socialist principle of "from each according to his capacity, and to each according to his need." It is the utopia that men and women yearn to live, a sign and anticipation on earth of the Kingdom God has prepared for the just.

We said good-bye to the people in the communities with embraces and tears. The following day the children went back to school, and the peasants returned to work in their fields with the hope the corn would continue to grow and offer an abundant harvest. One of the members of the coordinating commission said:

"It's painful for us to separate, but it also brings us joy for the hope that your visit gives us. From this day forward, the army encirclement of our communities has been broken, offering us the hope to live in peace, without bombings or strafing, with the freedom to move and reunite with our families, and the chance to trade with other communities."

The CPRs represent hope and encouragement for many in Guatemala, in Latin America, and in the entire Third World. For that reason we must redouble our efforts and gestures of solidarity with the Communities of Population in Resistance, so that the flame of resistance will not be extinguished.

The Dark Night Of Resistance: Pastoral Work In The Ixcán

by Ricardo Falla, S.J.

Like the Communities of Population in Resistance (CPRs) in the Sierra, the CPRs in the Ixcán Jungle were formed during the 1980s by indigenous communities that had fled from the military repression and taken refuge in the jungle. One of the persons who accompanied them in their exodus was Ricardo Falla, an anthropologist and Jesuit priest.
Falla is the author of numerous books, including Massacres of the Ixcán Jungle, *which documents the military massacres of the early 1980s, and* The Story of a Great Love, *published by EPICA. The following article narrates his experience of pastoral accompaniment among the CPRs in the Ixcán Jungle.*

To some people it may seem impossible that pastoral work can be done among people who are in resistance. How can the word of God be preached as bombs fall? How can a network of catechists be formed in the midst of war? How can a living church grow when the people constantly have to flee?

In the following reflection we want to describe how we have developed pastoral work in the Communities of Civilian Population in Resistance (CPRs) in the Ixcán region of Guatemala. We will begin by describing the basis of this pastoral work, which is accompaniment of the people in their experience of persecution.

The idea of accompaniment is inspired by the way of following Jesus. Jesus tells us that anyone who desires to follow Him must take up His cross and walk behind Him, because as we follow Him in suffering, so also we shall share with Him in the glory. But today we do not see Jesus in the flesh even though He is risen. We only see Him in our brothers and sisters, who are all people, but especially the persecuted and the poorest.

Therefore, if we want to follow Jesus we have to follow our persecuted brothers and sisters to the limits of our strength, both physically and spiritually, to follow them with all our heart, with all our mind, with all our soul and with all that we have. This is the root of accompaniment by a priest and by the Church that does pastoral work among people in resistance.

The Pastoral Work of Accompaniment

First, accompaniment means staying with the people in their isolation from the rest of Guatemala. Six military posts form a crescent that presses the communities of resistance against the Mexican border; there also is a seventh military post, that of Cuarto Pueblo, that is placed like a threatening island in the middle of this area. The people cannot transport their produce to Guatemalan markets, neither their magnificent black beans, their abundant corn, their sesame and rice, their soya, nor their hogs and chickens. Neither can they visit their relatives and friends.

The Church also experiences this isolation because it isn't possible to send catechists to evangelize or celebrate with neighboring communities, nor to receive support from these communities. The people of the CPRs in the Ixcán are confined to a small area, and only with great effort and at great risk is it possible for people to cross the area where the military posts are located in order to ascend into the mountains to visit their brothers and sisters in the CPRs of the Sierra.

These communities have been the most isolated from pastoral attention until very recently. The priest is like the missionary of the past because he is cut off from communication with other areas and unable, for example, to communicate with the pastoral team in Xalbal, which is only a day's walk away, because of the military's presence.

Sharing the Anguish of the People

Second, accompaniment means not only experiencing isolation, but also experiencing the constant threat of attack that the people experience every day. We live under a gigantic jungle canopy, always hidden and always alert for the sound of an approaching helicopter that could spot us. If one leaves clothes to dry in the sunlight, it is necessary to stay alert so that they can be gathered up if the buzz of those deadly giant birds is heard. If the people are sowing, they have to leave the area where they are working if a warplane approaches.

The sky is a constant source of threat during the day and is equally so by night—mortars explode like rays of light in the darkness. These threats are always on the edge of one's consciousness; even when there is a dance or a mass, everyone must always be alert for the sounds of planes that the people in the CPRs can detect five or ten seconds before someone who is not used to the sounds can hear them. This constant sense of threat wears you down without your realizing it.

The people of the CPRs contrast their lives with the lives of the refugees because the refugees can live tranquilly, in spite of the sadness of being in exile. The priest and the catechists should be present and should not be leaving frequently because then the people will lose their sense of identification with them.

To See God in the People

Third, accompaniment means not only sharing the constant sense of threat, but also experiencing the army's attacks on the people. During periods when the army is carrying out special offensives, such as the six months at the end of 1987 and the beginning of 1988, these attacks are constant, whether by aerial bombing or by infantry troops.

In ordinary times these attacks are limited to the weeks when the army invades the area. For example, during the last weeks of November and early December 1992, the army razed three communities with the objective of "cleansing" the area that borders on the land where the returning refugees have settled *(Polígono 14)*.

During these weeks, the catechists and the priest, like the rest of the people of God, had to flee from the soldiers because the soldiers were going to burn whatever they found and no one knew whether they intended to capture people alive or kill them. Uncertain about what the army would do, we fled.

This may have given the army grounds to accuse the people of being guerrillas. But if we had stayed and the army had killed us, as happened in 1982, we would have committed the serious error that those who were massacred ten years ago committed.

As a result of these times of flight, which can last one or two weeks, an intense bond develops between the priest and the people. People respond with great affection, and give the priest the best food they have, literally taking it out of their mouths. I wrote in my diary on November 30, the day following the burning of the community, "Flor gave me an egg for breakfast, one of the few she had left, because her husband wasn't able to save even one chicken; she gave the other members of the family only half an egg. By the time I realized what her gift was, there was nothing left for her."

These things, which seem insignificant, are really of great significance to the pastoral mission of accompaniment. There is nothing complex about it. It is the simplest thing, but very profound, because the people see in me Jesus Christ, while I try to find Him in them. For what is pastoral work, if it is not making God present?

Jesus is Born in the Mountains

Being present among people who are in resistance is the basis of our pastoral work of accompaniment. But we cannot simply be present and stay silent. We have to provide the nourishment of the Word of God. Pastoral work is not only a matter of making God present in the midst of God's people; pastoral work is also leading the people to green pastures, providing them with spiritual nourishment that becomes strength for life.

But the Word of God covers a very broad range of themes. What do we choose as the key points out of this enormous richness? The answer is simple. We center on Our Lord Jesus Christ, on His life, His passion, His death and His resurrection. For pastoral reasons, that is to say, for reasons of basic pedagogy, we focus on the New Testament rather than preaching and studying the Old Testament.

The mystery of God is opened up by the Word of God present in the life, death and resurrection of Jesus. We emphasize this at all levels—children, young people, women and men—always trying to put the Gospel in a new and fresh light.

But someone may ask us, "What texts do you use most and how do you apply them?" More than texts, the people's resistance and the cycle of the year have led us to focus on three principle experiences from the New Testament: the birth of Jesus, his death and resurrection, and the coming of the Holy Spirit at Pentecost. The dramatizations of Scripture we try to do if we are not under attack help us a lot.

In regard to the mystery of the birth of Jesus, the most obvious aspect that the people in resistance apply to their own experience is the context in which Jesus's birth happened. It was similar to the situation we are in today. The Child is born away from his home, in the mountains, hidden, just as many children in the CPRs are born while the people are fleeing from attacks against their communities by the army.

"Are there any of you who have given birth during emergencies?" we ask in the women's classes. Someone always tells her story and this story is listened to with particular attention by the women who are pregnant, because they may have the same experience.

All the women, who have many children, identify with Mary's plight when she fled with Joseph to Egypt to escape Herod's decree to slaughter the children. They draw strength from Mary's suffering when they, too, must flee, carrying their young. What happens during these forced flights is something described elsewhere in the Gospel: there runs through the women's minds the curse, the scream or who knows what to call it, that goes, "Would that we had not given birth!"

The Passion and Resurrection of Christ in the People

Many comparisons can be made between the death and resurrection of the Lord and the experiences the people of the CPRs are living, because the people have witnessed terrible massacres and have survived. But where is the resurrection? Some people have objected that in my book *Massacres in the Jungle* I have said that I am announcing good news, but what can be good news about massacres?

But the people in resistance recognize the good news. The resurrection, they say, is that we are alive, and, even more, that we are in a process from which we are certain to emerge into the light of day and to be recognized as civilians—with all the rights of civilians—not only by the people of Guatemala, by the Church and by international solidarity, but also by the Guatemalan government.

The force of Jesus' resurrection overcame the soldiers, who fell on their swords when the rock rolled away from the sepulchre. We even have a song about this marvelous event to the tune of "The Morning is Joyful." The chorus goes: "In the middle of the night the soldiers were on guard so that no one could steal the body of Jesus. But he overturned the stone and shook the earth, rising with a great light."

Pentecost and the Birth of Community in the CPRs

In regard to Pentecost we are assisted by the intense experience that the people in resistance in the Ixcán lived during the years before the massacres. They had participated in the charismatic movement, which in essence was a very joyful experience. Although there were some distortions in the charismatic movement, it was undeniably an authentic experience of the Spirit.

The most essential point we draw from the account of the coming of the Holy Spirit is a comparison between the communal organization of life both in the early Christian Church and in the communities of people in resistance.

The CPRs very much resemble the communities of the apostles and the first Christians, since in the CPR communities life is egalitarian and very communal.

Everyone has basically the same food to eat. While each household cooks in its own way according to the culture of the ethnic group to which the family belongs, and the variety of foods is supplemented by each family's own garden, still all the people have their basic food supply assured and corn is distributed equally according to the number of members in the family. Thus, either everyone goes hungry or no one goes hungry. There are none of the great differences that cause jealousy, violence and prisons.

In the early Christian communities, described in the Acts of the Apostles, it does not appear that there was collective production; but their communal spirit serves as an inspiration to the CPRs to encourage this form of collective production, which has been the nucleus of their resistance.

Much of what I am saying is critical of the military. But pastoral work among people who are resisting the persecution of the army cannot be otherwise, since the soldiers persecute us and want to kill us, and burn our houses and cut down our cornfields. How can pastoral work not be antimilitaristic if it seeks to provide spiritual nourishment to the People of God?

What nourishment are we going to give them? Are we going to tell them to surrender to the army? What did Judith say when the leaders of her besieged city gave God a deadline in which to save them? She raised her voice in protest, because they were showing a lack of trust in God, because instead of encouraging the people to resist they were suggesting the idea of surrendering.

Resistance is understood, in the context of our pastoral work, as a gift of God, and, therefore, as a gift that must be received freely; thus, if individuals don't want this gift wholeheartedly, we tell them that it would be better that they leave. Resistance is also understood as a struggle for life and never as a struggle that is suicidal, fanatic or isolated from reality.

The people in resistance, in spite of the suffering they have experienced, are very down to earth and psychologically very healthy, probably because they have succeeded in overcoming their suffering through their heroic faith. If our pastoral work has been able to help nourish this faith, we pastors have also felt ourselves to be very satisfied and happy.

The Hour Of Indigenous People In Chiapas, Mexico

by Bishop Samuel Ruíz

On January 1, 1994, an event occurred in Chiapas, Mexico that changed the face of history, not only in Chiapas, but in Mexico and beyond. For the first time in five centuries, a rebellion of indigenous people broke through the silence that had shrouded the indigenous reality and catapulted the world of indigenous people onto the world stage. One of the elders from the indigenous communities explained what had happened this way: "The hour of indigenous people is beginning on our continent. This is our hour, not three days from now, but now. We are the womb of the continent." And while the Church in Chiapas was not directly responsible for or involved in the rebellion, the seeds of participation, inclusion, and dignity had been sown by it during the past three decades to lay the foundation for a truly indigenous Church in Chiapas.

Samuel Ruíz, the bishop of the Diocese of San Cristóbal de Las Casas, Chiapas, Mexico, has worked with indigenous people for the last 35 years. Since the rebellion he has served as mediator of the dialogue between the Zapatista rebels and the Mexican government. Recently, he resigned from that position. He gave the following talk March 24, 1995, at the Central American University (UCA) in San Salvador on the occasion of the 15th anniversary of Archbishop Romero's martyrdom.

There have been many interpretations of the January 1, 1994 rebellion in Chiapas. First they said that foreigners were responsible for the conflict, because there were no guerrillas in Chiapas. Then, when they heard the guerrillas speak Tzotzil, Choj, Tojolobal—all indigenous languages—they said that the foreigners must have been in Chiapas for years. Even the guerrillas said they had been preparing themselves for a long time for this rebellion.

Finally they said that these foreigners were none other than the foreign nuns and priests of the Diocese of San Cristóbal de Las Casas, and they took all the names of priests they had denounced in the newspapers in past years. Now these nuns and priests were presented as the ones who trained the guerrillas in Chiapas.

It's important to realize that we are speaking of four towns in a coffee-producing region of Chiapas, where a third of the indigenous population had taken up arms. As time passed, there was talk of dialogue, and recognition of the fact that the indigenous people of Chiapas were fighting for a just cause. Some people even had the audacity to admit that one of the fundamental causes of the conflict had been a mistaken policy on the part of the Mexican government.

Everything for Everyone, Nothing for Us

I would like to publicly thank the international press today for their coverage during the first ten days of the conflict in January 1994. They covered it with great precision and understanding of the context. Thanks to this information and the ability of some journalists, who were accustomed to covering a war situation and penetrating the areas of conflict, we not only had a good source of information but a kind of "Truth Commission" that became a means of judging the events from outside.

One morning, just after the rebellion began, I received a call from the BBC in London asking me about what was happening in Chiapas. I had no idea what was happening. Within two or three days practically the entire international press had come to Chiapas. It was on account of this outside pressure that the war only lasted ten days, and a unilateral cease-fire was decreed.

Both the Mexican and the international press helped move the Mexican government to a point necessary for the establishment of peace. That's how it became clear that it was an indigenous movement, not only because the indigenous people of Chiapas constitute the majority of the movement, but also because the movement expresses indigenous perspectives.

Months later, an indigenous priest told me, "Bishop Ruíz, I'm the pastor of an indigenous parish, and I'm proud of my indigenous identity. I want you to know that once I discovered what this movement was all about, I understood that it expressed our indigenous thinking: 'Everything for everyone, nothing for us.' This is our way of being and our way of thinking."

Clearly, this is a just cause. In January 1994, the bishops of Chiapas published a document about the rebellion in Chiapas. We spoke of an understandable desperation given the state in which the indigenous people found themselves, without any other means of demanding justice except a violent one. At the same time we recognized that other indigenous people had demanded justice without resorting to violence.

As several indigenous people said, "Those who rebelled are our sisters and brothers, their cause is our cause, even though we have not chosen the path of violence." When asked why they had taken up arms, they replied, "Sir, I have not taken up arms, nor have many other indigenous people. But I ask you, would you still be talking to me if nobody had? Are we finally going to be heard, now that some indigenous people have rebelled, or are we going to have to wait another 500 years?"

An End to Violent Revolution

Something exceptional and unique for Latin America happened with the Zapatista rebellion. This was not a traditional movement that exclaimed, "There is no justice, we must take power to impose justice." Instead, the indigenous people were seeking a social explosion that would bring the people of Mexico to their feet; not to take up arms but to participate in a civic manner so that Mexico might form a transitional government and lay the foundations for real democracy.

The indigenous people did not want to take power, nor form a political party; they wanted to arouse the Mexican people who were not unaware of their oppression, but only discouraged. We thought, as did much of our continent, that it was no longer possible to bring about change; not even by violent means. We were all convinced that the violent movements in Latin America had come to a definitive end. They had—and have—no future.

What happened in Chiapas has no other explanation, I believe, than this: The international economic system, which is capitalist, is unchallenged today, now that the socialist bloc has disappeared. With the coming of automation to Mexico, the economic system not only marginalized the indigenous peasants, but the workers as well. Nobody had any hope for social transformation.

Double Oppression of Indigenous People

By any stretch of the imagination, it was impossible to think that the indigenous people of the continent would be able to raise up any hope for change, especially since they were so bound to their customs. Whenever there were programs of social change the indigenous people said, "We're not interested. We don't want to become inserted into the process of social change."

Many times people said to me, "Bishop Ruíz, don't you realize that the kind of pastoral work you are promoting is setting back the liberation of this continent? You want the indigenous people to become aware of their indigenous identity. But it's not their awareness as indigenous people but as people who are exploited that will bring about any hope for change. As long as you continue to insist otherwise, you are discouraging any possibility of change."

So when the indigenous, who traditionally have been opposed to any change, now began to speak of change, everyone was surprised. What happened is that indigenous people became aware of their double oppression. They realized that they were oppressed economically and they were oppressed culturally.

The Hour of Indigenous People

During the first days of the rebellion, the people of Mexico took action. They didn't come to Chiapas in the same way they had come 15 years before, when the Guatemalan refugees first crossed the border to seek refuge. Then we received visits from a few drivers who brought a few truckloads of supplies and letters of support from some parish or diocese.

Now we had visits from bus-loads of people who came to Chiapas and asked, "What do you need? What can we do?" Indigenous people from the entire continent—from Canada, the United States, from South America—came to tell us, "Your cause is our cause."

A Bolivian woman working in the United States told me the following story. A few days before the January 1 rebellion in Chiapas, she visited several communities of indigenous people from Oaxaca who were harvesting crops in the United States. She asked one of the young men, who had just finished school, if he planned to go on with his studies.

"No, I'm not going on. Why should I?" he responded. "We don't have any future." One of the elders of the community was sitting nearby, listening in silence, his silent presence a witness to the approaching disappearance of his people.

When the rebellion in Chiapas broke out, the young people of this indigenous community began to discuss what had happened, what they should do, and whether they should go to Mexico or remain in the United States. Some were of the opinion that they should remain in the United States.

That's when one of the elders lifted his voice and said, "You young people just don't understand what is happening. The hour of indigenous people is beginning on our continent. This is our hour, not three days from now, but now. We are the womb of the continent."

500 Years of Indigenous Resistance

After the rebellion broke out, a cease-fire was established and the dialogue began. It continued until the indigenous people told Manuel Camacho Solis, the President of Mexico's personal representative at the dialogue, the real problem: "Don't you understand that we don't want another school or another hospital? That isn't the problem. The Mexican law says that indigenous cultures must be respected, but it doesn't say the indigenous people even exist today, or that we are part of this country.

"We don't need more schools and hospitals. The problem is that the law continues to justify our marginalization. We are the original inhabitants of the continent, but we don't want to live by ourselves. We know there are many others and we want to share our country's future."

Perhaps this is one of the things that has never been understood. It's not only justice that is at stake. In 500 years nobody has been able to eradicate the indigenous people from this continent. The indigenous people are here and they are claiming their right to participate.

If you read their declarations you will realize that by "participation" they don't mean to participate on other's terms, but to offer what they have to give to the transformation of society in Mexico. The hour of indigenous people is beginning on our continent. This is their hour, not three days from now, but now. They are the womb of our continent.

The Indigenous Church In Chiapas: Bringing Heaven To Earth

by Gonzalo Ituarte, O.P.

Subsequent to the January 1, 1994 rebellion in Chiapas, much attention—both negative and positive—has been focused on the Church in Chiapas. In an interview with EPICA, Samuel Ruíz, the bishop of the Diocese of San Cristóbal de Las Casas for more than 35 years, offered this perspective on the process of doing liberation theology: "First comes solidarity and love of neighbor, in whom Jesus is present as a sacrament. As a consequence of this love, the neighbor's suffering becomes my own as well. There is an appropriation of suffering, motivated by love. Then comes the second moment, a struggle to change this suffering. Only then are we ready for the third moment which is reflection upon this love and struggle—that's theology."

Gonzalo Ituarte, O.P. is the Vicar General of the Diocese of San Cristóbal de Las Casas in Chiapas, Mexico. He has been a close collaborator of Bishop Ruíz for many years, and offered the following interpretation of the indigenous rebellion to EPICA just weeks after it occurred in January 1994.

Often, people ask us to comment on the events in Chiapas in light of liberation theology. Bishop Ruíz always responds, "What do you want me to say? That my theology supports revolution? We are more concerned about the option for the poor than about liberation theology. Our main concern is that the Gospel really becomes Good News for people now, and not simply after death." For 35 years, Don Samuel has been telling the world, especially the local and national Mexican government, about the situation in Chiapas. But very little has been done by the government to respond to the needs of the people.

The indigenous people are not treated as human beings. They are not recognized as Mexican citizens. Our pastoral work has been to let the people know their rights and their dignity. That work led to the formation of a very strong movement of indigenous organizations. For years the people have been trying to change their situation with no results. As a last resort, some of them began to prepare for the rebellion that surprised all of us as the new year began.

The work of the church in Chiapas is more than a theological effort; it is the gospel itself. The nonviolent option of Christ in the gospel is clear, and we support that; but we understand why the people have decided to take up arms. Our option for the poor has not changed. They are our brothers and sisters.

Our basic concern is how we can bring a little bit of heaven to earth. What does it mean for the will of God to be done on earth as it is in heaven? If the will of God is to become real on earth then we must not only call ourselves brothers and sisters, we must act like brothers and sisters. That's very difficult to do in a racist society like Mexico.

Even for the Church, indigenous people have always been at the front door, but they have never been allowed to enter and be fully accepted. There are ten million indigenous people in Mexico, but we still don't have an authentically indigenous Catholic Church. Indigenous people have to give up their identity and their culture if they want to be fully accepted in the church.

How does the government respond to the work of the church?

Usually politicians in Mexico don't listen "downwards," but "upwards." They want to tell the President what he would like to hear. That's what has happened here. The government didn't listen to Don Samuel, because he was looking downwards; he was seeing a different reality. The politicians were telling the President that Chiapas was a paradise.

The Spanish-speaking people, the very rich and the very powerful, have always controlled the lives of the indigenous people in our communities. Not many years ago, landowners owned tens of thousands of acres of land. Anytime they wanted, they could sell the land along with the indigenous people who lived on it. The indigenous people were part of the property. The landowners treated them as slaves, or as little children whom they could punish.

Most of the landowners were surprised by the strength of the people when they asked the government for title to the lands. Until 1992, Mexican law said that the land was communal land, and belonged to those who worked it. Now the land belongs to those who can pay for it.

We Make the Road By Walking

For the indigenous people, the land is much more than something to buy and sell; the land is their mother. When the indigenous people are preparing to plant, they first ask permission from the mother earth: "Forgive me, I'm going to hurt you. But we need the food that comes from you." Then they give thanks for the harvest. It's a sacred relationship. Nature is part of their lives. The new Mexican law invites the indigenous people to buy and sell their own mother. But for the landowners, land is a business.

You said that before 1992 the land was owned by those who worked it. What does that mean?

The law said that the land should be used to benefit those who worked it. But for many years the land reform law was not implemented properly in Chiapas. The land was concentrated in very few hands. In 1992, the laws changed. Before then, any land the Indians held they held in common, on land called *ejidos*. Each person had a certain piece of land, but they could not sell it. They could only pass it on to their children. That was the law. Now, if the majority of the people on the *ejido* agree, they can sell the piece of land they have. That will further concentrate the land.

Do you expect now that big companies like Nescafe will come in and simply buy all the land?

It's already beginning to happen, even with the worst indigenous lands. The indigenous people have to grow their corn on steep slopes, in the middle of stones, weeds, and sticks. They make a hole in the ground and put the seed in the hole with lots of fertilizer. They have no other choice. That's the land that nobody wanted, until now. There are some good indigenous lands in the jungle, and these are the lands that are being bought right now. It's a great problem.

What hope is there that the negotiations will succeed?

The peace process has to succeed. If it fails, we are lost. Not only be-cause we don't want a war—a war in Mexico would be terrible—but also because the poor would suffer, politically and physically. If the peace process fails, the war will begin again. I don't know who will start it, but I know who will lose. I think if we want to strengthen the peace process, we have to show that the commitment of the church is to the poor, using peaceful means. The official doctrine of the church does allow rebellion against unjust authority. And in other countries, liberation theology has been associated with revolutionary movements for change. But until now, we have never spoken of a just rebellion. Instead, we have spoken of love, brother- and sisterhood, and justice. We have preached the subversive power of the Gospel.

The real problem is that even with such a clear situation as the one we have here in Chiapas, of poverty, marginalization, and discrimination, nothing was ever done. Those who are really responsible for this war are the local authorities and the wealthy landowners who control the local government. Basically, what the indigenous people of Chiapas have been asking for is that the agrarian reform be applied; but they have been denied justice for 500 years.

So I think that if we want to maintain the trust of the indigenous people, we have to strengthen the commitment of the church to the poor. For too long the church has been committed to the rich, and that is what helped the local elites stay in power.

What support does Bishop Ruíz have from other dioceses?

Officially, the National Conference of Bishops has supported Don Samuel, and appointed six more bishops to help him. But they are not so enthusiastic. Basically their attitude is to try to balance and control. They are always looking for ways to soften the strong words of denunciation of Don Samuel. They say, "We don't support Don Samuel and his theology or his pastoral work. But we do support his work for peace."

I suppose they envy Don Samuel because the people really love him. He has been with them. Very few bishops in Mexico can say that they have visited all the communities in their diocese several times in 34 years, and in Chiapas there are thousands of communities.

Usually the bishops or the priests visit the landowner's house. The indigenous people would come to this house to receive baptism. When Don Samuel discovered the misery and the suffering of the people, he decided to visit the little houses of the people instead. That change was explosive.

"How is it possible that a bishop is going to visit the Indians?" the landowner would ask. "Is he not a person of reason?" For the landowners, the only ones who think are the people of Spanish descent.

Unless the Gospel is a threat to the wealthy landowners and politicians, it must be irrelevant, no? Even in the church there is a power struggle. In March, 16 archbishops and three cardinals will be appointed, and to be named an Archbishop or a Cardinal, for some clergy, is very important.

Don Samuel, however, has never thought of leaving this diocese. He's just looking downwards, and walking with the people.

IV

Defending
The Rights
Of
The Poor

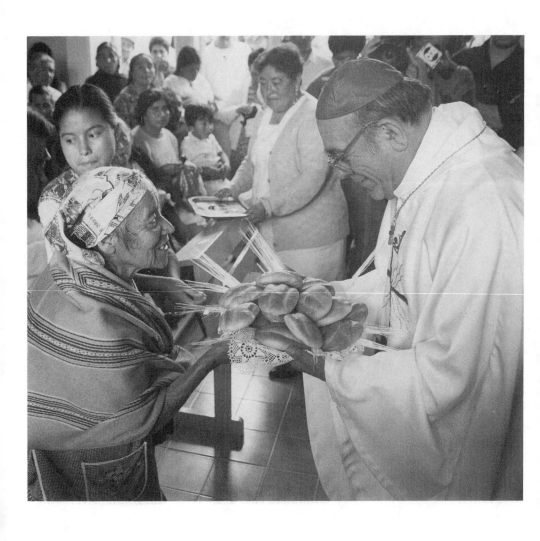

Poverty And Death: A Scandal That Cries Out To Heaven

from the Oscar Romero Pastoral Center

During each of the past three decades, the United Nations spoke of a "decade of development" in Latin America. Large sums of money were poured into the nations of the region, producing economic growth. But the masses of poor never saw the full fruits of this development. At the end of each period, the results were the same: the gap between rich and poor actually widened. One of the early voices in defense of the poor were the Latin American bishops at their conference in Medellin, Colombia in 1968. They spoke of poverty as a scandal that cried out to the heavens. This cry has not been silenced; on the contrary, poverty continues to be the greatest challenge facing the people of Latin America and the Caribbean. The following reflection is from the September/October 1997 edition of Letter to the Churches, published by the Central American University (UCA) in San Salvador and translated by CRISPAZ.

The United Nations recently published their annual report on poverty and human development. The report aims to be objective and to take note of all advances made in humanity. But in its entirety, it is devastating: "With globalization the rich are winning and the poor are losing." "110 million people in Latin America and the Caribbean live on less than one dollar a day." "The richest person in Mexico has a fortune of 6.6 billion dollars, equivalent to the combined income of 17 million poor Mexicans." And we could go on.

Two months ago, the Economic Commission for Latin America (ECLA) offered its own report. The absolute number of people that live in conditions of poverty in Latin America rose last year to 210 million, the highest level in the history of the region. While it is true that, in relative terms, the number of poor people dropped from 41 to 39 percent, it is also true that the absolute number increased. Economic reforms promoted by governments have not benefited the poorest of the poor.

The above figures should be public knowledge. They should be presented and explained by those who govern our countries. However, they remain practically ignored. Regarding the reality of our planet—of how more than six billion human beings live and die—we know infinitely less than we know about soccer and its stars, about soap operas and their romances, or about the music industry and its gold and silver records.

It could be said: "That's the way it is." And it could also be said that this is better than mutually killing ourselves as we do in times of war. The conclusion, then, would be that we are doing all right in the world. But this is not a convincing argument.

A Scandal That Cries Out to Heaven

There was a time in which the Latin American Bishops' Conference conclusions at Medellin and Puebla were frequently cited with conviction and commitment, without fear of being accused of "getting involved in politics," without fear of facing those that govern, military officers, and the rich. They were always cited with a great love of risk and the willingness to suffer persecution if necessary. And what did they say?

"This misery, as a collective fact, is an injustice that cries out to Heaven" (Medellin, 1968). "We consider the growing gap between the rich and the poor, when illuminated by our faith, to be a scandal, and a contradiction to being Christian. The luxury of a few becomes an insult to the misery of the masses. This is contrary to the plan of God and to the honor that it deserves" (Puebla, 1979).

In these documents, the Catholic bishops speak of "injustice," a word that is not used in technical reports such as those issued by the United Nations and ECLA. But the word is irreplaceable in describing reality. And if injustice exists, it is because there exists a structural sin.

It is also said that the reality of our continent is contrary to the plan of God. What the reports say in numbers and statistics is that "the creation of God is in very bad shape." Life, for which God created all human beings, is not equal for all human beings, and for thousands of millions it is a heavy weight that is almost impossible to carry. In making us sons and daughters, God also makes us brothers and sisters. The luxury of the few and the misery of the masses is a true insult to God.

We are not lacking someone to tell us that humanity is improving. But this provides little consolation. In the first place, it does not exempt from blame those who promote inequality, although they may see themselves as a necessary path so that the poor, little by little, in 20 or 30 years, can live a little better. In the second place, we must look at our tradition. The prophets of Israel were wise enough to know that in times of monarchy, the macroeconomic benefit was greater for the Israelites than for the slaves working in Egypt. But the possibility to "live a little better" did not hinder them from condemning as intolerable the situation of the poor in Israel.

Do we or will we "live a little better" with globalization? Realism and optimism are understandable attitudes and are to a certain point necessary. But something rises out of the deepest part of the human being demanding that we establish an absolute minimum criteria regarding life, equality and fraternity, such that those with everything cannot calmly repeat, "Don't exaggerate and don't complain, little by little we will live a little better."

What Have You Done For Your Sisters and Brothers?

We are not lacking someone to tell us, "There is not protest without a proposal for an alternative." To this we respond that we are not just protesting, rather denouncing. We denounce the concealment of reality and of the euphemisms that are used to describe it—"countries in development," "inequality," and "less opportunities" rather than underdeveloped countries, injustice and close to death. We denounce the fact that economic policies are not subject to ethical concerns. Is there no sin involved in configuring the world this way?

This could be the first contribution of the Church: To seek and to state the truth, to become a guardian of the world. In this way, the Church could also influence the collective awareness. The Church could encourage and demand political, social, and scientific forces to look for solutions or to take serious steps in that direction, and to religiously motivate and offer a meaning of life and happiness based on austerity, not opulence; on sharing, not selfishness. If the Church helps to promote this awareness, it will be a great thing for El Salvador.

But we have to put our hands to work. Since Archbishop Romero wrote his fourth pastoral letter in 1979, neither Salvadoran bishops nor the Episcopal Conference have provided a serious, well-documented writing about poverty and injustice in the country, with theological and socio-political reflection (though some bishops do attempt to talk about this in their declarations). They talk of other evils, of sin in general, but they do not begin with cruel structural injustice, the great sin against life.

The majority of pastoral directives do not confront poverty and injustice as a central problem, to say it kindly. This way of practicing Christianity does not encounter any obstacles from the hierarchy. But smaller groups do not act this way, they are concerned about justice.

The Church can and should do much in favor of justice in a fundamentally unjust country. But to do so, it needs credibility: to appear truly incarnate in the sufferings of the poor and to be prophetic, with honor and Christian charity, to those that generate, ignore, or conceal poverty. Unless we do so, we cannot present ourselves before a God that asks us: "What have you done for your sisters and brothers?"

Memory And Hope: Telling The Truth About Guatemala

Interview with Graciela Azmitia

During the past two decades in Guatemala, more than 150,000 people have been killed, and another 50,000 detained and disappeared by paramilitary death squads. Most of the violence, bordering on genocide, was committed by the Guatemalan military and paramilitary groups like the civil patrols against the largely indigenous population. Only in December 1996 were Peace Accords signed between the Guatemalan government and the URNG guerrillas, putting an end to more than 35 years of war.

Even prior to the signing of the accords, the Guatemalan Church began to document the effects of the violence through a project called, "Recovery of the Historic Memory (REMHI)." Human rights promoters interviewed more than 5,000 survivors concerning the violence and published their findings in four volumes entitled, "Never Again." Graciela Azmitia, a member of the REMHI team, was interviewed by EPICA in November 1997.

I work with a project called REMHI, which stands for Recovery of the Historic Memory. The name is significant, because what we hope to do is recover our history by collecting people's testimonies about what happened to them during the war in Guatemala. This allows people the opportunity to express themselves, begin to come to terms with the violence and recover their dignity.

The roots of the project go back a few years, when people began to tell their stories during confession in their local parish. In their confessions they told everything that had happened to them during the period of violence. That's when the idea came that the Church had to do something. REMHI was created and now works in ten dioceses in Guatemala. We have received testimonies from people about events occurring as early as 1960, and as late as 1996 when the Peace Accords were signed.

REMHI has four stages. The first stage began in April 1995, and was a period of sensitizing, training and organizing people to work with the project. We began a publicity campaign, and distributed pamphlets to people throughout Guatemala, inviting them to participate in the project by voluntarily giving their testimony. We also initiated little radio programs to explain why we must not forget the past.

Stage two was the actual collection of testimonies. The promoters went to the parishes, or the houses, or wherever people decided they wanted to talk. There are 600 people in our team, 500 of whom are Maya Indians. One third are women, and more than half are under 35 years of age.

The third stage—the stage in which I am working—consists of processing the information. Our job is to read the testimonies as they come back to the Archdiocese in Guatemala City, and feed them into a computer data base. Then we do an analysis of the data, which will form part of the final report to be released in March 1998.

The fourth and final stage will be the effort to give the results of the project back to the people of Guatemala at the local level.

Who are the people who have given testimonies?

Those who give testimonies are the victims of the violence, people who have not been able to speak during all these years. They are the witnesses. Already we have documented 5,300 testimonies in which people tell what happened to them, and how they suffered violence. We have testimonies from every part of Guatemala, from urban as well as rural areas. It is significant that many testimonies were recorded in a local Mayan dialect—of which there are 23 in Guatemala—since many people do not speak Spanish. That's why we made an effort to reach out to the rural communities. This in turn provided many people with the opportunity to voluntarily give their testimony. And not only victims, but also the perpetrators of the violence have offered testimony.

How did you decide to get involved in the REMHI project?

I am also a victim of the violence. I felt it was important to speak out so that everybody could learn the truth about our history, and so that we don't repeat what happened. That's why I decided to participate in REMHI. I wanted to tell what happened to me, and also to know what happened to other people.

What kind of work do you do with the project?

I am part of a team of people whose job it is to read testimonies from the massacres that have occurred. Since we began working, we have had to read anywhere from 1,000 to 1,300 testimonies. I am in charge of analyzing the testimonies that deal with the massacres in the Petén and in Huehuetenango.

Is there one testimony in particular that impressed you?

What made the greatest impact on me was a testimony about a massacre that happened in Petenac, Huehuetenango. The person who gave this testimony survived the massacre, and later told what he saw: they killed the men, shot them in the head, and then burned the bodies. They shut the women and children up in a school, threw grenades at them, and burned their bodies. Young women were raped, then tortured and killed.

This happened in 1982. The killing began at 8 a.m. and lasted until 5 p.m. when the army left. It was a battalion of 500 soldiers. What most affected me was what this witness saw when he returned to a hill that overlooked the school. As he was climbing, he saw a river of water, but it wasn't water—it was the melted fat from the bodies that were being burned.

When I read that I began to cry. I even had nightmares the next night. What made an impact on me was not only the written testimony, but also the cassette tape I was listening to, because I could hear the survivor crying as he told about the children being burned alive. It was horrible to hear all this.

There is also a testimony about another massacre that happened in Dos Erres, El Petén. But this one was told by one of the perpetrators of the violence. Several groups of the army participated in this massacre. This particular soldier was a cook for the Kaibiles elite battalion. I was the person who transcribed his testimony. He told his story like this: "In the beginning, it was hard for me to participate in these massacres, but later I got used to it, and I even enjoyed it." It's as if he lost his conscience, or lost any appreciation for life. But I think he must have had a guilty conscience, otherwise why would he give his testimony about how he became involved in participating in these massacres?

Could you share what happened to you during the war?

Yes, my father, my sister and my brother were all kidnapped and disappeared in September 1981. My father was personal secretary to Cardinal Mario Casariegos for 38 years, and worked for him in the cathedral. My sister was 23, a teacher, and director of a literacy project in the department of El Quiché. My brother was a first-year student in the university. He was 22, and like so many students was accused of being a communist. That's why they were kidnapped: my sister because she worked with the literacy project, my brother because he was a university student, and my father because he had information about the church. My brother was the first to disappear. Later they kidnapped my sister, and finally my father.

When my father was taken away, my mother, my little brother and I were with him. A car with tinted windows and no license plates stopped us in the street, four armed men got out of the car and ordered us to stop. When this happened my little brother and I ran, but my mother stayed with my father. The men told her, "Señora, you have nothing to worry about, nothing will happen to your husband." But we knew we would never see my father again.

To this day we don't know what happened to him, where he is, where they took him or what they did with him. We know nothing. My mother managed to find a convent where the sisters looked after her. She had a nervous breakdown, and was unconscious for two weeks. They sedated her and took care of her until she was able to cope. For those weeks I had no idea what had happened to my father or my mother. Later they told me. I had gone to hide with my little brother in the house of a schoolmate. We remained in hiding for one month, until we were reunited with my mother, and people helped us escape to Mexico where we lived for 11 years. I was 16 years old at the time. I came back to Guatemala five years ago.

Why do you think it's important to make these testimonies public?

First of all, so that we know our own history. Not everybody knows what happened in Guatemala so we need to reveal the truth. And we also need to begin a process of forgiveness. Once we know the truth we can begin this process. If we know who was responsible for the violence we may begin to forgive them, try to rebuild our communities and live in peace.

But is it really possible for the victims of the violence, simply by knowing the truth, to feel a desire to forgive? Especially if those responsible do not ask for pardon?

Our hope is that when we bring the results of the project back to the communities, sooner or later those responsible will recognize their culpability. But until that happens we the victims can begin the process of forgiveness. It's very important to us as victims to forgive. But it's also important to say that forgiveness does not mean there is no justice. There must also be justice. So the process of forgiveness is very slow. It's going to take years. Still we have to begin to work to educate people for peace.

What do forgiveness and justice mean to you?

It would mean that I learn the truth about who was responsible, and that they were truly sorry about what they did, before there could be forgiveness. The words of the Lord's Prayer, "Forgive us our trespasses as we forgive those who trespass against us," must be more than just words. Because I am a Catholic, for me the most important thing is for the people to stop committing acts of violence and repent of what they did.

It may also be that forgiveness is not possible—especially if the other parties are not sorry for what they have done. If they do repent, however, it means that they accept their culpability privately and publicly, that they accept the punishment which justice requires, and that they pay their debt, no?

Did what happen to you and your family happen to many Guatemalans?

Yes, in fact much worse things happened to others than what happened to me. Since I began to listen to other testimonies I've realized how much other people have suffered just to survive. They went for days with nothing to eat. Many died of hunger or cold as they fled to the mountains to escape. In the rural areas entire communities were attacked by the army. The violence in the city was more selective, and was directed against leaders. That's why a lot of people in the cities never realized what was happening. They created a climate of terror in Guatemala. That's why so many of us have had to remain silent. Now, however, it's time for us to speak out.

So the results of these testimonies are going to be published?

Yes, in March 1998 the results of the REMHI project will be published. This will be the fourth and final stage of the project, to give back to the communities the information that they gave us. Only now it will include an interpretation of our history.

Will these efforts to tell the truth make a difference with respect to military impunity?

We Make the Road By Walking

Our final report will make clear what part military impunity has played in the violence. We hope that by publishing the testimonies that impunity will begin to diminish. But impunity has been a fact of life for years, and it will be difficult to change it overnight. What the REMHI project does is offer people a way to speak out, so that the truth will be known and impunity will begin to lose some of its force.

What about reconciliation on a community level? Are there any communities where this is taking place?

The process is very slow. It won't happen overnight. But, yes, there are communities where agreements are being made. One of the goals of the REMHI project is to educate our people for peace. The fourth stage is when the work of reconciliation will really begin. REMHI will sponsor meetings, workshops, forums and trainings as a way of bringing the results of the project back to the local communities. There will be pamphlets and posters to help in this process of education for peace. We are also preparing skits in the local dialects of the Maya people. There will be ceremonies, homilies, and monuments. REMHI is also involved in legal assistance to communities, accompaniment of the returned refugee communities, and mental health projects for the people and communities affected by the violence.

Do you feel that your participation in the REMHI project has helped you begin this process of reconciliation on a personal level?

Yes, very much so. I have found myself as a person in the sense that I am doing something now that I was unable to do before. I am able to channel any feelings of hatred or vengeance into something positive—helping other people. And in this way I am participating in the process of reconciliation in Guatemala. Perhaps I will never find my family, but I know that others will because of the work that REMHI is doing. This inspires me to work even harder, to have more hope, to have more faith. Reconciliation may be years away, but I still feel the need to begin the process of forgiveness. What gives me hope is to know that there are many people who really want to see something good accomplished. I believe that change must come some day. I pray to God for that.

The Rebellion Of The Excluded: Lenten Reflection From Chiapas

by Bishop Samuel Ruiz

*On the 4th Sunday of Advent, 1511, Fray Antonio de Montesinos de-
nounced the violence of the Spanish conquistadors and strongly defended the
rights of the indigenous people: "By what right and with what justice do you
keep these Indians in such cruel and horrible servitude? With what authority
have you waged such detestable wars against these people? Are they not
human beings? Do they not have rational souls? Are you not obliged to love
them as yourselves?" Sitting in the assembly was a young conquistador,
Bartolomé de Las Casas, who one day would become known as the Defender of
the Indians and the first bishop of Chiapas. Today, nearly five centuries later,
Samuel Ruíz has taken upon himself this role of defending the rights of
indigenous people in Chiapas.*

*On January 1, 1994, more than a thousand armed rebels—almost all of
them indigenous people—took over four towns and more than a dozen villages
in the southern Mexican state of Chiapas. With "nothing to lose, no land, no
work, poor health, no food and no right to freely choose our leaders," the
Zapatistas launched their rebellion. Six weeks later, negotiations between the
government and the Zapatistas began, and Bishop Samuel Ruíz, from the
diocese of San Cristóbal de Las Casas, in Chiapas, was asked to mediate. The
following homily was given by Bishop Ruíz during Lent, 1994.*

This year the Lenten season has a specially profound meaning for the
church of San Cristóbal de las Casas in Chiapas. The outcry over events
that have recently stained our lives with blood has led us to the "desert" of
prayer so that we may listen attentively to what the Lord is saying.

In Chiapas we are immersed in a war that has challenged the political
structures, on both a local and national level, and has shaken the conscience

121

of the entire Mexican society. It is in this context that we must live our Paschal experience so that we can truly pass from death to life and the resurrection that occurs in the history of our people.

As Christians, we can make a decisive contribution to this process of conversion, not only with our prayers, which are more necessary now than ever, but with our prophetic voice and our committed action for peace.

The Rebellion of the Excluded

In Chiapas, poor and indigenous peasants came to the momentous decision that they had no alternative but to take up arms. The Zapatistas say that most of their leaders are indigenous peasants. They are not foreigners nor are they violent professionals.

It is difficult to determine with precision their ideology. In their statements to the press they present a nationalistic and socialistic perspective, whose basic demand is justice for the poor. Their voice has had a great impact, precisely because it is the voice of rebellion of those who are excluded from the system, both indigenous and non-indigenous.

Nobody knows for sure what the military capacity of the Zapatistas is. At first, many people ridiculed how poorly armed they were. But soon their discipline and intelligence amazed everyone, including the Mexican army. The major strength of the Zapatistas, however, is not so much their military capacity as their ability to create sympathy for their cause in civil society.

They have become not only catalysts, but spokespersons for the generalized discontent expressed by civil society towards the established order. They have put forward proposals, and not simply denunciations, that have challenged all of us.

We cannot justify the decision to opt for violence as an ordinary means of resolving the grave problems of the region. We said this very clearly at the beginning of the conflict. But, as pastors of the church, we understand the anguish and prolonged suffering of our sisters and brothers that led them to conclude that all peaceful channels had been closed to them.

When the social order was disrupted by the armed insurrection of the Zapatistas, the Mexican army immediately intervened to establish order. According to the evidence gathered by the church, and corroborated by the national and international press and nongovernmental organizations (NGOs), the Mexican army committed violations of human rights against the Zapatistas and the civilian population.

These violations, which were carried out by the institution charged by the Constitution with guaranteeing the security of all Mexican citizens, offended the conscience of the nation. For that reason these violations must be investigated.

As a diocese, we have suffered the profound consequences of the armed conflict. We have consoled the victims, provided refuge to those displaced from their homes by the war, channeled humanitarian aid to the victims, defended human rights, and mediated the negotiations. In all these actions we have received support from other churches in Chiapas, and from the Bishops' Conference of Mexico.

The Roots of the Rebellion

The negotiations provide hopeful signs that a peaceful solution can be found. There are, however, indications that the storm is not over. An excessive control of the region by both armies has prevented the civilian population from moving freely in order to buy food, plant their fields, or seek medical care. Both armies have forced out the civil authorities that govern in the towns they control. This has made the peace process more difficult.

Some of the civil authorities expelled by the Zapatistas have found support among the powerful elites, who in turn have pressured the Mexican army not to withdraw from the region. The army has even organized paramilitary groups to threaten and attack journalists and members of NGOs.

The actions attributed to the Zapatistas have deeply affected the national conscience; but the actions of the Mexican army have had an even greater negative impact on public opinion. There is evidence that the army kidnapped members of the Zapatistas, and executed both prisoners of war and civilians.

Chiapas is one of the most impoverished states in Mexico, but not because it lacks natural resources for development; on the contrary, it has them in abundance. Nor is the problem of underdevelopment due to the fact that most of its population is indigenous. Chiapas is poor because of the unjust structures of an economic model that has systematically enriched a few people at the expense of the majority.

These structures institutionalize violence and daily threaten the social fabric, sowing the seeds of popular rebellion, both political and armed. Faced with the violence of the established order, the church cannot remain silent without being in complicity with the sin of the world.

With all the energy the spirit of the prophets and the Gospel gives us, we have demanded the conversion of the people and the transformation of social structures. But it appears that we have only been a voice crying in the wilderness.

We Make the Road By Walking

Our Historic Debt to the Indigenous Peoples

The situation of Chiapas has become even more complicated in the last few years. The gains of the 1917 Mexican Revolution—land reform, public health, social justice, universal suffrage, and public education—never reached us. The structural adjustment program, which was imposed on us by the current Mexican government in order to further integrate Mexico into the capitalist bloc of the North, only made it easier for private interests to control the resources of the countryside.

The indigenous people feel abandoned by the Mexican government. The powerful and wealthy elites allied to the government have stripped the indigenous communities of their land and their products with total impunity.

Last year, in our pastoral letter, "In This Hour of Grace," we concluded: "We have to speak out about the present economic system that oppresses us. The wealthy need two things to be able to continue this path of enrichment: privatization, and the North American Free Trade Agreement (NAFTA). These two things are necessary for capitalism to continue to benefit wealthy and powerful investors, both Mexican and international; in turn, this new economic model marginalizes thousands of peasants and workers."

The armed rebellion of the indigenous people of Chiapas has demonstrated that Mexico has a historic debt to pay to the indigenous peoples. Throughout Mexico's history, indigenous people have never been taken into account by government projects. They have been considered a superfluous population and a hindrance to national development.

From a global perspective, the indigenous peoples are the forgotten and marginalized peoples. They are strangers in their own land. This is the greatest social sin for which all of us should ask pardon. The exclusion of the indigenous peoples is a historic error that the rebels throw in our face, and for which we must make amends.

We cannot continue to build the Mexico of the future on the graves of indigenous peoples, nor can we ignore the most ancient roots of out national identity. Indigenous people are the descendants of the original inhabitants of our country, and they deserve to be treated with dignity.

The rebellion of the indigenous people has been a catalyst for the generalized discontent of other social sectors. As a consequence, Chiapas has generated solidarity from distant and diverse groups. The indigenous people are saying to the leaders of Mexico that it is not valid to exclude them by thinking only of the sectors of the population that are considered the most productive for Mexico.

The most serious challenge now is not the dialogue between the government and the Zapatistas. The solution to the armed conflict will not termi-

124

nate the grave problems of the country. What is even more crucial is the solution to the discontent of civil society. Mexico cannot remain the same as before the rebellion in Chiapas.

The Resurrection of Our People

The Lenten season is a call to recognize personal and structural sins, to mend our ways with concrete actions that go to the root of the problem. We must prepare ourselves to contribute the best we have to offer to this new day that will lead us, after the suffering of the cross, to a glorious resurrection of our people today.

For that to happen, the land that was stripped from the indigenous peoples must be restored. Development projects and programs must make the interests of indigenous people, and not profit or economic and political productivity, a priority. The best guarantee for any public or private investment must be the strengthening of peace and social concord.

Civil society has played the principal role in making dialogue and political negotiation possible in order to resolve our conflicts. We must keep this critical awareness and combative spirit of the people in mind, as we try to bring to a fruitful conclusion the dialogue for peace, and guarantee that the peace accords are fulfilled.

We must open paths of political participation for everyone to help build a new Mexico that will eradicate the structural causes of violence and respond to the ancestral and legitimate aspirations of our people.

This is what Christians understand as the Paschal experience of passing from death to life, both as persons and as a people, in order to "structurally" place ourselves in the path that leads to the resurrection today. The resurrection of Christ in our people reaffirms and anticipates our hope in the final resurrection.

But these aspirations for resurrection that we all share will not have any historical expression unless we commit ourselves in all seriousness to its realization in the life of our people. We must be prepared to accept the way of the cross, with dignity and courage, and pay the cost of the pain and suffering that the construction of peace will surely require. As followers of Jesus we do not seek martyrdom, but if that is the price we must pay, we accept it as the radical consequence of love for our neighbor.

Defending The Poor In Panama: The Aftermath Of The US Invasion

An Interview with Father Conrado Sanjur

Just after midnight on December 20, 1989, the United States sent 27,000 troops as part of an invasion force to Panama in its largest military action since the Vietnam War. The US Army used highly sophisticated weapons against unarmed civilian populations; 442 bombs were dropped over civilian areas during the first 13 hours of the invasion. More than 2,000 people died.

The invasion was strongly condemned by both the United Nations and the Organization of American States (OAS) as a violation of international law. The invasion also raised questions about whether the United States would comply with the Panama Canal Treaty which requires the United States to turn over the Canal to the Panamanian people December 31, 1999.

Father Conrado Sanjur is a Panamanian priest and Chair of the Coordinator for Human Rights in Panama (COPODEHUPA), a nongovernmental organization defending the claims of those affected by the 1989 US invasion of Panama in a case before the Inter-American Human Rights Commission of the Organization of American States. He is also Executive Secretary of the Central American Coordination of Christian Base Communities. He was interviewed by EPICA in 1996. This interview appeared in the Summer 1996 edition of Challenge, *EPICA's quarterly magazine.*

The December 1989 US invasion of Panama may have accomplished US objectives, but it was a tragedy in economic and political terms for the Panamanian people, especially the poor. Many things are still unresolved. For example, a full accounting of lives lost has yet to be made; and those who lost homes and businesses have never been compensated, either by the Panamanian or by the US government.

According to the Torrijos-Carter Treaties, the US military bases should be withdrawn from Panama by the year 2000. We trust that those treaties will be honored. Nevertheless, we are concerned that both governments want to renew negotiations about the US military presence in Panama. For example, in September 1995, President Pérez Balladares and President Clinton announced they would begin exploratory talks for a renegotiation of the Panama Canal Treaties.

The talks were scheduled for November 1995 and then postponed so that there could be a national debate on the question. The government hasn't said very much about the talks lately, but we believe that it is actually beginning a process to extend the treaties and US military presence in Panama.

Our position is that there should be no further negotiations about the bases. We have undertaken a broad popular education campaign in Panama regarding the need for the United States to completely withdraw its military bases. We're also starting a broad public debate about the topic because the Panamanian government is conducting its business in a secretive manner.

In addition, we are attempting to address the problem of toxic wastes caused by the military bases in Panama, something neither the Panamanian nor the US governments want to deal with seriously. We believe that an exhaustive, truthful, objective study needs to be made of the actual extent of the toxic waste deposits. We feel that with the full military withdrawal there should be a decontamination of those sites, since they are the direct cause of the problem.

There are many reasons to justify a definitive withdrawal of the bases. It would open up a whole new horizon for Panama's future. The lands surrounding the canal and occupied by the bases are the most potentially productive lands in our country. These areas should be converted to civilian use and open the way for the Panamanian government to implement policies of social and economic development for the country.

We need to point out that both past and present Panamanian governments have supposedly committed themselves to modernize the economy. At the same time, we see a deterioration of basic human rights. One sector that has been affected throughout Panama's history is the indigenous population. There is a great deal of tension right now because the Panamanian government has granted mining concessions on lands belonging to indigenous communities. The government has utilized repressive measures, not only against indigenous people but also against workers who demand their rights.

We would like to ask you to give attention to these concerns. Specifically, we are calling for support around these demands: first, complete withdrawal of US military bases and clean up of toxic wastes; second, the legal

127

claims made before the Inter-American Commission on Human Rights by the victims of the 1989 US invasion of Panama; and third, solidarity with the struggle of indigenous communities to affirm their self-determination and right to their lands.

How does the United States benefit from maintaining its military presence in Panama?

Supposedly, the United States wants to remain in Panama because its presence here enables it to carry out its war against drugs and drug traffickers. But the military bases actually contribute to drug trafficking because they are a major source of drug consumption. We believe the supposed war against drugs is really a new way for the United States to maintain geopolitical domination of the region.

And what benefit if any would this continued presence offer to Panama?

Panama gains nothing from the US military bases on its soil, neither economically nor in terms of military defense. On the contrary, we need their removal so that the Panamanian government can take responsibility for guaranteeing projects on the lands that economically benefit the Panamanian people. The current struggle in Panama over these lands is whether they will simply benefit the transnational corporations or whether they will benefit the Panamanian people by becoming a pole of social development for the people and generate housing, employment, health care and nutrition.

How did you first come to work with the victims of the 1989 US invasion of Panama?

This has been a very interesting process. A few months after the invasion, a group of families from the neighborhood of El Chorrillo came to our offices in COPODEHUPA. El Chorrillo was the neighborhood that was most severely damaged by the invasion because it was where the general barracks of the Panamanian Defense Forces were located.

El Chorrillo is an extremely impoverished, marginalized neighborhood, with a population that is largely black. When the invasion occurred, thousands of houses were set afire leaving some 20,000 people homeless, and killing or wounding thousands. Many people were profoundly traumatized by the invasion and continue to be so today. These consequences have never been redressed by either the Panamanian or the US governments.

Prior to coming to our office, the families from El Chorrillo went to the Panamanian government to denounce what had happened to them in the invasion. They were told by the government of President Endara that Panama could do nothing, that the United States had carried out the invasion. The US Embassy also refused to address their grievances.

Finally these families came to COPODEHUPA and we put them in contact with the Center for Constitutional Rights in New York, which is the office that is officially representing them before the Inter-American Commission of Human Rights of the OAS. The case calls on the United States to recognize its responsibility for the invasion and to pay indemnities to the families who suffered as a result of the violence.

The case was formally submitted to the Inter-American Commission on May 10, 1990 by the families from El Chorrillo to be compensated for damages resulting from the US invasion. This is the first case that the Commission has ever agreed to decide that has been presented by a group of civilians. Normally cases are presented by governments of countries. In 1993 the Commission formally adopted the case for judgment; the last session was in 1995; we expect a final decision to be made in September 1996 [the decision is still pending as of September 1998].

So none of the victims has received any compensation for losses incurred during the invasion?

Absolutely nothing.

You also mentioned your work with indigenous communities. What are some of the challenges they face today in Panama?

One of the problems in Panama's history has been the complete violation of human rights with regard to indigenous communities. According to the Church in Panama, the indigenous are the poorest of the poor, especially one group, the Ngobe-Bugle. The other indigenous communities live in similar conditions, but the Ngobe-Bugle are the most mistreated and most marginalized.

The indigenous people account for about eight percent of the Panamanian population. The largest group, the Ngobe-Bugle, are actually two tribes that number about 123,000 members and live in the provinces of Bocas del Toro, Chiriquí and Veraguas in the western part of Panama. Two other communities, the Embera-Wounaan, number about 18,000, and live in the province of Darien in eastern Panama. A fifth community, the Kuna, number about 47,000, and mostly on the San Blas islands off the northeastern coast of Panama. All of these indigenous communities live in similar conditions.

There's no getting around the fact of racial discrimination in Panama. There is discrimination against blacks, there is discrimination against indigenous peoples and against peasants. It's a fact. It may not be noticeable, but in practice there is no racial equality in Panama. These sectors are socially and economically marginalized.

The discrimination against blacks is primarily racial, and it fosters attitudes of contempt and racial inequality. Blacks in Panama live mostly in the city of Colón in the North, and in Panama City in the South. Many of them came from the Antilles Islands in the Caribbean to work on the construction of the Panama canal. Many live in the poorest neighborhoods, like El Chorrillo in Panama City.

In the case of indigenous people, in addition to racial discrimination, they suffer a denial of their right to self-determination and to the lands on which they live. The land is closely linked to the culture and social organization of indigenous communities, as is the environment. It's not only a question about the right to work the land, but about the right to live in harmony and unity with the natural environment.

What response does the Church in Panama have to these problems?

One of the characteristics of the Church in Panama is that it is very similar to the Catholic Church in other Latin American countries. The Panamanian hierarchy is by no measure prophetic; it is committed only to assisting the poor, but not to addressing the fundamental problems of the country. The Church is fearful of popular movements for social change and it has traditionally regarded them as violent and subversive.

But there are exceptions. The bishop of Colón, for example, has been concerned in recent years about the problems of black people, indigenous people, and women, since these are problems that he faces in his own diocese.

The neighborhood of San Miguelito in Panama City, where I work, has traditionally been a place of innovative pastoral projects. Priests from the Archdiocese of Chicago helped lay the groundwork for Christian base communities there during the 1960s even before Vatican II and the Latin American Bishops' meeting in Medellin in 1968. They developed a model of church that responded to the problems of real life in the world, and they promoted the participation of lay people in the church.

Their work had political repercussions. It helped organize the people into small groups and social sectors with their own autonomy, and even their own local government. When Torrijos came to power in Panama, he sympathized with the experience in San Miguelito and proceeded to multiply the model of organization on a national scale. The original movement, however, retained its pastoral, liturgical and theological dimensions.

The theology of liberation teaches that it is precisely in our encounter with the poor that we encounter God. But we have to seek out this encounter with the poor, we can't avoid it or romanticize it. The poor want to exercise their right to be recognized as human beings and to be treated with dignity. They want to be participants in changing society.

This is the liberation that the poor are seeking, and this is also what the Gospel teaches. The Beatitudes of the Gospel can only become real with the participation of the poor. The Kingdom of God belongs to the poor, and the poor should be able to exercise their right to cooperate with God in making the Kingdom a reality. If the Kingdom is not realized it is not because the poor are not capable of collaborating in its construction, it is because there are powerful forces opposing it that deprive the poor of any voice.

Archbishop Oscar Romero of El Salvador used to say that the Church must be "the voice of those without a voice." This is very important, but we must always remember that it's not that the poor are not capable of speaking for themselves; if they no longer speak it's because they have been silenced by someone.

The Panamanian people do not expect much from the United States. We have received too much from them already! But we know how to distinguish between the people and government of the United States. We have had too much experience with the US Embassy, the US government, the US invasion, the US military bases, and too little experience with the people and churches of the United States. I think it is essential for both the people and the churches here to understand the true situation of the Panamanian people.

The situation of Panama is different from Central America, but there is also much in common. The condition of workers, peasants, indigenous communities, students and children is the same as in Central America. Because there were strong and hopeful movements for change in El Salvador, Nicaragua and Guatemala, Costa Rica and Panama were always the last in line. Now we share a certain equality in terms of the current situation in the region. There is little difference in how neoliberalism affects our peoples. We see the same signs of the time.

V

Women Transform The Face Of The Church

Seeds For
A New Planting:
The Church
In Nicaragua

by Indiana Acevedo

*A popular Nicaraguan folksong spoke about Christ being born, crucified
and resurrected in a little Nicaraguan village, Palacaguina. For many Nicaraguan Christians, the identification of Christianity with the revolution was so
strong that the words of the song might as well have been true. With priests
heading up government ministries, thousands of Christians among the
Sandinista martyrs, and tens of thousands of Christians participating in
Sandinista projects and organizations, Nicaragua seemed to be the meeting
ground between revolutionary faith and Christian faith. With the defeat of the
Sandinistas in the 1990 elections, however, Nicaraguans reappraised this
marriage between the two.*
*Indiana Acevedo, a lay Catholic, is one of hundreds of women who
functioned as leaders of the Christian base communities in Nicaragua. In the
following reflection she shares lessons learned after more than a decade of
work with the base communities.*

In the late 1970s many young people, including myself, joined Christian
base communities. Through these communities we began to understand that
the Gospel called on us to respond to the political situation in which we were
living. We protested Somoza's rule of the country. We peacefully occupied
churches, we took over vacant land, we demonstrated against bus fare increases. At that time it was a "sin" to be young since young people were so
identified with the struggle. Because we protested, we suffered persecution
and many clandestine graves of young people were discovered.

In 1978, a year before the triumph, I joined the Sandinistas. From then
on, my faith has motivated me in my political work with the Sandinistas and

in evangelization within the Christian base communities. I've never experienced conflict between doing political work and doing base community work. They're different, but they're not contradictory.

Political work—discussion and action—is more straightforward and can be accomplished more quickly. It is much easier than Christian formation because it lends itself more directly to an analysis of the situation in which people live. Therefore, leaders are formed more quickly. You can train a political activist—if the person is sharp—in six months.

Working in Christian base communities, on the other hand, is a slower process. The Bible, not political analysis, is the basis for raising people's awareness. Forming leaders in the base communities is a much slower process in which people discover what the Church is, what it means to belong to the Church, and what our response as Church should be.

I consider myself an activist within the Sandinista party, but as an individual, not as a representative of my base community. The Sandinistas have respected my decision to work in the Christian base communities. "Religious" thinking doesn't limit my political work, and working for the party doesn't keep me from working with the Christian communities.

At times I and others in the base communities have had problems because people in the neighborhood see us doing political work and claim that we're not really Christians. Most people still do not understand the integration of faith and politics, so they get confused. In their minds, a person may be either religious or political, one or the other, but not both. Even within our Christian communities, some members say that we are "political" as if because of our political convictions we shouldn't work in base communities, too.

If my faith were not well-grounded, I might say, "Okay, let them belong to their base community and I'll do my political work." That would be easier. But I have strong convictions. Therefore I still belong to my base community and, no matter what others say, I'm going to stay, because the witness of my participation, the witness of my presence, is what is going to convince them that I have truly made an option for the Church of the Poor.

The Elections: What Went Wrong

After the Sandinista defeat in the elections in February 1990, our people were very demoralized. At first we blamed ourselves for what happened. However we came to realize that the Sandinistas lost not just because of our mistakes but because of the low intensity war against our country, the military draft, and the economic situation—people had to eat. We gave ourselves a little breathing space and reflected on what had happened. We tried to understand how we, the Christian base communities, had fallen short of our hopes.

Looking back, we can identify some of our mistakes. As leaders in the base communities, part of our work was to analyze our reality, but our focus was more often on the material rather than on the spiritual side of defending life. This was reflected in the way we tended to choose political language rather than Biblical language.

We also made mistakes in our methodology. We would choose a Bible reading we considered appropriate for the political situation at the time. We often read from Exodus about the journey of the people of Israel out of Egypt or from Nehemiah about those who kept watch and worked and prayed (Nehemiah 1:4-11). We often used the Gospel reading from John (John 15:13), the one about there being no greater love than giving your life for your brothers and sisters, a passage that meant so much to us when young people were killed in the *contra* war.

These were all very important readings. Through reflecting on them, we wanted the people to become more committed. But as leaders we erred. We tried to be the one who interpreted the reading in light of the political reality instead of letting the people themselves make the connection. People with a traditional faith, who are often the very poorest, can only do this after a long process of practice and discovery. We were too impatient.

Now we are trying to recognize our mistakes and to learn from the people. We have changed our method of Biblical reflection. Instead of reading the Bible and applying it to the situation we are experiencing, we read the Bible and try to understand it within the context in which it was written and to let interpretations of its meaning and its relation to the current situation come from the people. Our plan now is to respect the process people must go through, even if it takes years.

Another problem was that we often found ourselves only responding to emergencies because every day brought new ones: thirty people killed by the *contras*, threats from US imperialism, planes invading our territory. We did everything we could to respond to the latest crisis but in the long term this didn't leave us time for spiritual growth and for deepening our faith. Our work in formation and conscientization suffered.

The Church of the Poor: A Political Project?

Over the past ten years the base communities have experienced many changes. However, the fact that many people do not understand the relation of faith to politics has made our efforts to build a Church of the Poor more difficult. Some people criticized the base communities' identification with the Sandinista government and projects. Just because as leaders of the base communities we understood the relation between faith and politics, that didn't mean that the people understood.

After the Sandinista victory, many members and leaders of the Christian base communities suddenly took on jobs as Sandinista political activists or as officials in governmental ministries. They became absorbed in revolutionary tasks and didn't have time for their base communities or Biblical reflection.

For those of us who stayed with the base communities, our work changed. Now a revolutionary government was in power, which responded to the people's aspirations. Before we had our own projects for community development; now we supported the projects of the revolution. We lived out our faith by supporting the revolution as it developed under the leadership of the new government.

For example, we joined the government's literacy project wholeheartedly. It was a project we needed because we wanted people in our communities to be able to read the Bible. All of the catechists who could read became literacy teachers. We identified with government projects like the literacy campaign and the vaccination campaigns and the building of parks and clinics; we didn't want to set up parallel structures for community development. As base community leaders, we didn't see any contradictions between the revolution and our Christian faith. I can't say that I identify totally with the political project of the Sandinistas, but as a member of a base community I identify with those projects that give life.

It's one thing, however, to recognize where there are problems and another to say specifically what else we could have done. Realistically what option was there other than to support government projects? Basically we didn't have any other options. Our work was for the poor and it was the government that was leading the way.

We carried out some projects independently of the government, but not many. For example, five years ago the coordinators of the local Christian base communities were concerned about forming leaders so we started a school of Christian education. People receive Christian formation and they learn about the Bible, politics and the social sciences.

Through experiencing all these difficulties, we've come to accept that as the Church of the Poor, we are a minority within the Church. We've grown, but very modestly. In consequence, because there are few of us, we have to work hard. We have very limited economic and material support. For example, since 1979 there are three hundred new poor barrios in Managua. Of these three hundred communities, we only have a presence in eight and even there our work is limited.

New Challenges Facing the Church of the Poor

In August 1990 we concluded our regional assembly of all the Christian base communities in this region and agreed on three objectives for our work: accompaniment of the people; more pluralism in our pastoral work; and deeper reflection on our identity as Christian communities. By accompanying the people, we mean raising their spirits and strengthening their hope. We do this through our work and presence in the poor neighborhoods.

In regard to a more pluralistic approach to pastoral work, we have realized that the base communities alone do not constitute the Church of the Poor. The Church of the Poor is much broader and involves sectors of the Protestant Church, reflection centers and theological institutions, and all progressive Christians who don't identify with the hierarchy.

In striving for more pluralism within our movement, we must find a way to overcome the negative consequences of having been condemned ideologically by the bishops. The Catholic hierarchy has said to us, "You are not part of the church. You're an arm of the Sandinistas. You're atheists. You're communists." The hierarchy has bombarded Nicaraguans with this message, and for a people whose faith is very traditional, this has had a profoundly negative effect. For the people, the Archbishop of Managua is like God.

I believe it's necessary to re-initiate a dialogue with the Catholic hierarchy. We had grown tired of going to the bishops to ask for a dialogue, only to be rejected, but maybe it's time now to knock on the door again and hope for an opening. Maybe we can reach an understanding with the bishops without sacrificing our identity as the Church of the Poor.

In regard to reflecting more deeply on our identity as base communities, we are asking what it means for us to identify ourselves as the Church of the Poor. We maintain firmly that we belong to the Church and that we are not a separate or parallel church, which is the accusation the institutional Church makes against us. We have opted for a new way of living our faith, but we are not another church.

In the base communities we start with the Gospel and this leads us to commitment. Our understanding of faith is not limited to homilies, hymns and prayers; rather we combine prayer and Biblical reflection with action. What we offer is the opportunity to discover the Gospel and to deepen our faith. We teach not only that God exists, but also that God expects something of us. God wants us to treat all people as our brothers and sisters. God wants us to show solidarity towards them.

For the majority of Nicaraguan people who are very traditional and other-worldly, it is hard to become involved in the base communities. People are not used to the demands inherent in a commitment to social justice.

Responding to the Gospel

In these ten years of revolution it has been impossible to eradicate the whole legacy of Somocismo. Now the same economic policies are being implemented again. Ten years ago, we succeeded in tearing down the barbed wire. Now they are trying to confine us again, but I don't think they will be able to do this easily. They are going to put up the barbed wire, but we'll find openings. The people of Nicaragua have had ten years of freedom and have tasted power. We have experienced what it means to be human beings. We have learned to speak and it will be very difficult to silence us again.

As the Church of the Poor, we've worked against the current; we've worked at the edge of the institutional Church because we've been condemned by the hierarchy. We work on the margins of parishes or outside them. We work exposed to the wind and the burning sun, on the edge of everything with almost no resources. We work with our fingernails; we don't have—as the hierarchy does—large amounts of money to hold retreats, to give food to the people, to transport people to and from worship, or to give people religious materials. So what do we have? Only the Bible and a willingness to work and to build a Church responsive to the Gospel of Jesus.

Our Eyes Were Opened: A Mayan Woman Speaks

by Elena Ixcot

As in Nicaragua and El Salvador, the poor in Guatemala began to organize to defend their rights. The Church played an important role in this process, helping indigenous Christians awaken to their dignity. In the highlands of Huehuetenango, El Quiché and the Verapazes, for example, local churches set up cooperatives and trained indigenous Christian leaders in areas where peasant groups successfully organized. These communities were later targeted by the Guatemalan military during the 1980s and more than 440 indigenous villages were destroyed.

In the following testimony, Elena Ixcot shares her journey of faith as an indigenous Christian. Elena and her husband Felipe are Mam Maya from the highlands of western Guatemala where they were farmers. Elena attended school for three years, Felipe for four. They fled the violence in Guatemala in 1982 and received church-sponsored Sanctuary in the United States. Their story was published in the July 1990 edition of Challenge, *EPICA's quarterly magazine.*

The women of our village would meet every Sunday afternoon to study the Word of God. We studied the biblical texts that were read in the morning mass in order to deepen our understanding about what God asks of us. Through this, we learned that the word of God is not just a history of past events, but that the Scripture is being relived today.

Little by little, our eyes were opened, and we began to understand more clearly the world in which we lived. This led us to organize our women's group better. The group kept growing until there were more than 125 women participating.

The first project we undertook was home visits. For example, we would visit sick people, people in jail and couples who were having marital problems. We didn't make these visits because we felt sorry for the people. Rather, we felt the pain of our brothers and sisters as though it were our own.

Our husbands also had Bible study meetings on Mondays and Fridays. Every month they held a retreat with catechists from other villages. They shared their experiences and told about the work they were doing in their communities.

As a result of the meetings, our husbands organized themselves to help with the farm work of those families who were falling behind because someone was ill. The men would take turns. Some would prepare the fields for planting, some would sow the seeds, some would do the weeding, and others would harvest the crops.

If someone in the community died and the family was poor, we would contribute a little money—even though we were poor ourselves—to help the family with the burial of their loved one.

Our husbands would help the grieving family with their farm work. Despite the difficulties of our lives, it gave us joy to live in our community. We also belonged to cooperatives that helped the women with weaving projects and taught the men better ways for planting.

It would take the whole afternoon to tell you all our experiences over the years. The most important thing, however, is that our reflection on the word of God is what gave us a new consciousness.

A New Theology of the Poor

We grew while living under brutal repression. Our reality was and is characterized by hunger, theft of our lands, high infant mortality, ever increasing poverty, repression and death. Those of us who work on the big coffee plantations or in factories are seen by the rich as nothing but objects who produce wealth for them.

For those of us who are poor, the word of God is the history of liberation, not only liberation of the spirit, but also liberation of the body. A human being is made of flesh and blood as well as the spirit. The apostle Paul tells us that our body is the temple of the Holy Spirit. If that is true, then why do we allow this temple to be trampled on by those who want to use us to make profits? This is one of the questions that people began to ask in our community.

As we thought about questions such as these, I and many other Christians began to awaken. This was true especially for us women, because we are even more marginalized and discriminated against than men are. We are seen as animals that are dangerous to society. No one wants us, and we are like foreigners in our own country.

For example, when we go to sell our products in the public markets, the police abuse us when we don't have any money to pay for licenses and taxes. It is the same in the hospitals. They treat us with contempt just because we are indigenous and because we wear our traditional clothing.

In the courts, too, when we come to ask for justice, they won't listen to us just because we don't speak Spanish well. Instead, they make fun of us.

The government has started campaigns of forced sterilization of the indigenous people. This is a policy of extermination. This inhuman campaign is carried out by the Ministry of Public Health and is paid for by the United States government.

As if this weren't enough, the government counterinsurgency policy means special suffering for indigenous women. Every day government soldiers rape women in the villages and the soldiers are never punished.

In the face of all of this, which we call a "project of death," we have come to understand that being a Christian means following Christ and committing ourselves to the Gospel of Christ. We believe the true Gospel is a message of justice, of brotherhood and sisterhood and of life.

We believe that people shouldn't be at the service of theology, but rather that theology should serve the people. We don't believe, as do many people, that religion can be separate from politics. To us, this is absurd and alienating. How can you separate the soul from the body?

Why We Are Hungry?

Many people are scandalized when Christians participate in a liberation process. They say that we are getting involved in politics. But we have a different vision and interpretation of the word of God than people in other countries, especially the rich countries. In rich countries, the majority of the people throw food—which to us is something holy—into the garbage. In our country bullets and bombs are the daily bread of our people.

Those who make money from religion and politics, like the fundamentalist sects that are sent to Guatemala by rich people in the United States, constantly put into our people's heads the idea that those who don't have food, don't have it because of bad luck or because they have sinned. Those who have food in abundance and enough to waste, they say, have it because of the goodness of God.

These are not the real reasons why many Guatemalans are hungry. In Genesis 1:26-28, God tells us that the land belongs to us all. But in practice God's will is not carried out. The rich descendants of Europeans in our country and the rich in other countries, through companies like United Fruit, have seized the wealth that belonged to our Mayan forebears.

So while Guatemala is a land rich in cattle, people die of hunger. Meat is exported to the United States, as are our sugar, our bananas, our coffee, our cocoa, our cotton and our oil.

Today we are beggars who see from a distance others planting our lands. Now there is no longer a place to plant corn and beans, which are holy to us. The Mayan bible of our grandparents tells us that we were made from corn. Without corn, we feel lost; without corn we feel sad.

The dream of every Maya is to have a piece of land on which to plant corn, because corn gives us spiritual enrichment; corn gives us physical resistance; corn gives us strength and health. Through corn we sing. Through corn we laugh and sigh and cry. Through corn our lives are formed and we are born. To strip us of our land for planting corn means to kill our people and culture.

A Cry for Freedom

The time has come for a people who for centuries have been oppressed and ignorant to rise up. We are claiming our rights based on the word of God in the Holy Scripture.

Neither suffering nor death can silence our cry for freedom and our hope for resurrection and life for all our people. We believe in dignity and justice and the liberation of the poor. If historically the Church erred in favor of the rich, now we ask it to allow us to possibly err also, but on the side of the poor.

In achieving liberation, some of our people will lose their lives and shed their precious blood. Sixteen Catholic priests, both Guatemalan and foreign, have been murdered. Twelve Protestant pastors have been murdered, 60 more have been kidnapped, and 45 have been "disappeared." Thousands of lay Christians have also been killed. These are not events of the past but experiences we are living today under a civilian government.

We are all the body of Christ

To be in solidarity with others is to feel the pain and death of our brothers and sisters in our own flesh. God asks us, "Who is your brother?" People who are not in solidarity will answer, "I don't know. Am I my brother's keeper?"

The Church cannot be neutral in the face of persecution. There will be a day when God tells us, "The blood of your brother Abel cries out to me for justice." (Genesis 4: 10)

Solidarity means putting into practice Christian communion. Because "when one member suffers, all the rest suffer and when one member is honored, all rejoice, because we are all the body of Christ." (Corinthians 12:26-27). While there are people who continue to live in misery and to be exploited, and while the massacres and killings continue, no one can rightfully claim to be a Christian without suffering alongside those who are persecuted and without sharing their hope for resurrection.

International solidarity is very important and your role is crucial. There are thousands and thousands of people in the United States who don't know what is happening beyond the borders of their country and they have the right and the obligation to know. Our struggle is your struggle, too.

Drinking From Women's Deep Well In Honduras

by Eliselda Guardado and Lastenia Méndez

*During the 1970s and 1980s, many women in Central America, Mexico
and the Caribbean actively participated in the popular movements for justice
and liberation in their countries, both at the grassroots as well as leadership
level. But it is only with the past decade that women's issues and a gender
perspective on broader issues of social and economic justice have truly
emerged as important struggles in themselves. This phenomenon has also
emerged within the reflections and concerns of Christian base communities.
Questions of economic opportunity, political participation, domestic violence,
sexual education and gender equality are concerns that men and women in the
base communities address with increasing frequency.*

*In the following reflection, Eliselda Guardado and Lastenia Méndez—
delegates of the Word and part of the San Isidro parish women's pastoral team
in Tocoa, Honduras—reflect upon the Gospel story of the Samaritan woman at
the well (John 4:1-26). They were interviewed by Jennifer Casolo. This
reflection was first published in the Fall 1996 edition of* Challenge, *EPICA's
quarterly magazine.*

Eliselda: We often read the Bible in a superficial way. We never stop to
think what these readings are really trying to tell us. For example, take the
passage about Jesus and the woman at the well. Who was this woman?
She's a prostitute with five husbands. Jesus said to her, "The man you are
with now is not your husband." Our reflection might end right here with this
statement unless we sit down, listen, and reflect on the story step by step.

Jesus came and sat at the edge of the well because he decided to draw
near to us women. He came to the well because this is a place where people

who are thirsty come. The well signifies a place of our hardships here on earth. Just imagine how many personal hardships women would be able to pour into that well? In every walk of life you always hear about what is happening to men, but never to women. You never hear about our many hardships, pain, and suffering. Each and every one of us has a well filled with life's bitterness and worries.

The Samaritan woman never would have imagined that Jesus would come and speak to her at the well. After all, she was a sinner! Jesus and the woman belonged to neighboring rural villages, but they were considered enemies because of their religious affiliation. In addition, women were discriminated against and did not belong anywhere, so Jesus' encounter with the Samaritan woman was a real surprise.

This woman is discovered by Jesus; he acknowledges her capacity as a woman, as a human being. She does not refuse to give water to him, even though she is a Samaritan and he is a Jew. Instead, she tries to discover the meaning of this encounter. She asks Jesus, "How do you know so much about me? Are you more powerful than our ancestors?" She realizes that Jesus is not just anybody. He knows about our whole life and teaches us that we're not alone.

We all have a mission to accomplish in life, filled with trials. Jesus himself was confronted with serious tests and trials. To know God is to look for God within our sufferings.

But who are those who suffer? Where is God today? God is in every woman that suffers, in every woman that lacks opportunity, in every woman that is not able to go out to buy a pound of sugar. All human beings were seen as equal in the eyes of Jesus. Once we discover this Jesus in our lives, we are able to give opportunities to others and see their capacity.

Women have been oppressed throughout history, yet the very same women have made it possible for men to succeed.

We Want Women To Become Aware of Their Dignity

Lastenia: Jesus made no distinction when he spoke to the Samaritan woman. The woman at the well was surprised to have Jesus speak to her. She was an imperfect woman! I wonder how her life compares to ours today? Even though we may not have five husbands, we have at least five problems that we face.

Eliselda: Perhaps she had husbands who were irresponsible, who beat her up, or who were extremely jealous. When I was a child I wanted to start working, but my father was completely opposed to the idea. Unfortunately, women are taught to obey men's orders, beginning with their father, their brothers, and their husband.

Lastenia: This pattern continues throughout life. Once we find support, we realize what life is all about. As soon as we recognize that the life we have with our abusive husbands is not the one we should have, that's it! Jesus wanted to take the blinders off the Samaritan woman so that she could really see. He told her that she wasn't being treated right.

Eliselda: Imagine how wonderful that was! Jesus told her all about her life. She said to him, "You are a prophet!" The Samaritan woman had discovered something about herself because she was touched by his wisdom. She finally felt that she existed.

Once I started to discover these things myself, I thought, "I'm finally out of a deep hole." Now, whenever I speak to anyone about this I say to myself, "I finally have a life, I'm alive!" That's why I don't like to hear women say, "I can't do anything, I'm no good."

If we were to sit down to think about what we have learned as part of a women's group, we would discover so much. By doing this we would understand how and why we do what we do. Deep down we know we do it to offer other women the same opportunity we had to get out of the house and do something positive with our lives. Our goal is to help other women become aware of their dignity, just like the woman at the well did when she spoke to Jesus. We try to do the same.

Women today are faced with the same difficulties as the Samaritan woman in the Gospel. Then, a woman was not allowed to speak to a man unless he was her husband. Today women still feel threatened and uncomfortable in that situation. Many women still feel that if they gather the courage to speak to an all-male group, the group simply won't listen.

It has always been extremely difficult for me to speak before a group, no matter how many times I do it. But then I think of the woman at the well and about her five husbands. I don't have five husbands, but I do have 500 worries on my mind. After so many attempts to convince myself that I'm no good, and that I can't do anything, my impulse is to listen to my inner voice that is telling me differently. Sometimes I feel the desire to leave this group. But deep down inside a thought comes to mind, namely, that God is saying to us, "Just do it!"

Lastenia: I don't think men mean to make us feel this way. If they hurt us, it's because they are ignorant and don't know any better. They haven't gotten to know God yet!

Eliselda: Men suffer because all the responsibility is on them, and taken from women. They find themselves at the end of their rope, unable to cope.

Men are coming to the conclusion that it's impossible and unrealistic to survive without the cooperation of women.

Lastenia: One woman said to me, "It's wonderful to see these women whose husbands allow them to work outside the home." Another woman said to me, "Someday I'll be able to join your group." These women are clearly thirsting for something, but they don't yet know how to satisfy their need.

Eliselda: The beautiful part about this Gospel passage is that it tells us there is water available for every one of us, women and men. Jesus offers this satisfying water so that we don't have to search for it in a deep well.

Lastenia: He offers us water that helps us feel alive, water that produces something positive in us. Only after drinking this water will we feel fresh, free, and true within, like the Samaritan woman at the well.

Biblical Reflection From A Mexican Village

Testimony of a Base Community Member

Christian base communities are often the place where the poor discover that they have a voice, and that their opinion is important. This is underscored by an anecdote from a elderly grandmother in El Salvador, who said of Father Rutilio Grande, the first priest to be martyred in that country: "He was the first person to ever ask me what I thought." Within a base community reflection, everyone is encouraged to participate. Real life concerns are shared, Scripture is read, people respond in concrete ways to the problems at hand, and the community's faith is celebrated. Weekly reflections, monthly meetings of group leaders, workshops on specific issues, quarterly assemblies, commemorations of the martyrs, participation in marches—all form part of the fabric of the base communities. And women are among the most strongest leaders and the most faithful participants.
Carolina is an active participant in the Christian base community movement in Cuernavaca, Mexico. She also works with Alianza Cívica, *a Mexican organization of civil society set up to monitor the elections. She was interviewed by Kim Erno, a Lutheran pastor who spent seven months with his family working at the Cuernavaca Center for Intercultural Dialogue on Development (CCIDD) in Cuernavaca, Mexico. Her story first appeared in the Fall 1997 edition of* Challenge, *EPICA's quarterly magazine.*

My parents were peasants who worked very hard. They didn't know how to read and write. They used to get all of us up to go to Mass at 5:00 in the morning. On the days that the Christian base communities met, they would come home at 9:00 or 10:00 at night. I saw their example of commitment, and one day I said, "I want to be part of the base communities, too."

I started to get involved with a group of parents of children that were going to receive their first communion. After the year of preparation was over, I realized that my daughter couldn't go through with first communion—not because she wasn't prepared, but because I wasn't! So the two of us stayed on for another year of preparation. By the time my daughter received first communion, I was well integrated into the base communities.

A Base Community Meeting

Base communities are small groups of people that meet to reflect on the problems they have in common and to hear the Word of God. They are called Christian base communities because they are related to the Church and because they are made up of humble, simple, poor people. Normally, we start talking about some happening in life, something going on in the neighborhood, in the country or even in the world.

We pick one thing to talk about, like the recent elections. Then we find a Bible reading that will help illuminate our situation. Those of us who are leaders encourage everybody to participate. First we ask, "What does this reading say?" and then, "How do we relate this to what is happening in real life?" Finally, we move on to some kind of a commitment. We have to start with very small commitments, like coming to the next meeting or inviting others to attend. We close with a little evaluation and maybe some refreshments. If there are no refreshments, we'll at least end with a song.

When the base communities were getting started in the 1970s, one of the local unions was protesting because the company was going to lay off lots of workers without any kind of compensation. There was a strike and the people from the base communities started taking food and water to the strikers, or going to sing a song with them. Some of the priests supported us, and of course our bishop, Don Sergio Mendez Arceo, did also.

I was still young when this was going on, but I remember that Don Sergio came to visit a group in the chapel. He saw that a young man was coordinating the meeting and was very concerned about helping the strikers. He was impressed how people united to support the striking workers, and how profound their reflections were on the Word of God.

Base Communities: Integrating Faith and Life

During the recent elections in Mexico, we read the passage from the Gospel of Mark where the disciples fight over which one will be first in the Kingdom of heaven. Jesus told them to become servants to one another. I like that passage because it shows that if the authorities really want to respect the people, they need to put themselves at the service of all people.

For example, there is a lot of concern in our community about education. It is very expensive. So we asked some of the candidates to pass a law to make education truly free. Supposedly it's free now, but the books that the government authorizes are so old, the teachers have to supplement them with newer books, and they ask the parents of the students to pay for them. Everything is very expensive! We want the government to come up with more efficient materials so that everybody can have an opportunity to learn.

Participation in the base communities has gotten people to be more involved politically. When my daughters see that I'm working with the *Alianza Cívica*, they say, "Well, why shouldn't we get involved, too?" My husband is also participating.

A lot of people from the communities lead catechism classes or premarital talks in the parish. There's also a parish health ministry where people visit the sick in the neighborhood and see what needs they have. When there is an emergency there is always solidarity. People here are very poor. Some live in cardboard shacks. If strong rains destroy their home, the neighbors organize and start to collect money so that they can build another little shack. We see all of these things as ministries, not obligations.

This is the difference between people from the base communities and others—we get involved. Some people dedicate themselves only to prayer and say the rest is politics. The base community people make the link between the two: faith and life.

Neoliberalism and NAFTA

Recently I attended a workshop on neoliberalism. We were looking at the whole issue of the North American Free Trade Agreement (NAFTA). It seemed like a very important issue for us to look at. We started to see that the Presidents of our countries are like referees in a soccer match. They are in the hands of powerful people who tell them, "These are the rules of the game. Make sure they are followed." But who is supposed to follow these rules? We are. They are the ones that break the laws, but we have to follow them.

We learned that the economy of Mexico is now in the hands of 14 families. And every day there are millions more that don't have enough to eat. Unemployment is going up, more workers are being laid off and more people are selling their wares in the streets. This is what NAFTA has brought us. It's sad to see that children still die of diarrhea when the government says the economy is doing really well. We don't even have vaccinations for children who live in our remote areas. And we're not even talking about Chiapas. I mean right here in Morelos!

If there is a government project for poor people, it ends up providing us with very little and costing us a lot in interest. People aren't interested in getting loans anymore because they know their harvest will not yield enough for them to make their payments. The number of children whose labor is exploited has increased. We don't need to go out and gather lots of information. We can see it on every corner. Children are cleaning windshields, selling gum, selling flowers, becoming human flame-throwers or juggling to make a little money. All this is the consequence of neoliberalism.

People tell us, "You can't change the world." And it's true, we can't change everything. But if there are little groups and more little groups of people in lots of places, then maybe we can do something. There's a line from a song that I like a lot. It says, "A day will come when we lift our eyes and see a land of freedom." But it also says, "Maybe neither you nor I will see this beautiful day, but we have to work so that it can one day become a reality."

VI

The Church
Of the Poor
In The
Caribbean

Freedom Is A Constant Struggle: The Church In Haiti

by Chavannes Jean-Baptiste

Haiti, like Central America and Mexico, has provided fertile ground for the convergence of faith and life, Christianity and politics, Christian base communities and popular movements for justice. During the 1970s, church-based centers formed hundreds of cooperatives and trained thousands of peasants in the essentials of the cooperative movement. Working on the premise that social change comes from the bottom up, grassroots organizers helped peasants all over the country form gwoupman, *a local group of 15 peasants, who farmed the land together and protested the harsh economic conditions and large landowners that exploited them.*

One of the leaders of this movement is Chavannes Jean-Baptiste, who was born into a peasant family near the town of Hinche in the Central Plateau of Haiti. In 1973 Jean-Baptiste went to work as an agricultural trainer at the Emmaus Training Center for Catechism and Agriculture in the village of Papaye. There he began a process of reflection and action with the peasant farmers in the area that laid the foundation for the Papaye Peasant Movement (MPP) with which he worked. Jean-Baptiste served as a cabinet officer during the administration of President Jean-Bertrand Aristide. Currently he is a cabinet office for President Rene Preval. His story appeared in the Fall 1993 edition of Challenge, *EPICA's quarterly magazine.*

When I began to work with peasants in the Central Plateau in Hinche, it soon became clear that the problems of the peasants were not mainly technical, but rather rooted in injustice and exploitation. Most peasants had to pay high rents or share their crops with absentee landlords. The Haitian government taxed the farmers heavily, but gave almost nothing in return. Moneylenders and grain merchants grew rich, taking advantage of the peasant's hunger.

I concluded that technical and social problems had to be considered together. During the next ten years hundreds of peasants were trained as organizers, teachers, and development workers, and new agricultural cooperatives were formed. These groups formed the basis of the Papaye Peasant Movement (MPP).

In 1987, the First National Peasant Groups Congress was held in Papaye; a year later the first MPP Women's Congress was held. By the time of Jean-Bertrand Aristide's election as President of Haiti in December 1990, MPP had more than 2,500 groups and 35,000 members. In March 1991, MPP formed the National Peasant Movement of the Papaye Congress, increasing the number of organized peasants to 100,000.

Six months later the military coup took place in Haiti. Soldiers based in Hinche attacked the MPP office. They arrested members and beat them. Eventually the military destroyed all the organization's property, and stole the peasants' corn. More than 3,000 MPP members were forced into hiding outside the Central Plateau. Today, the MPP continues its struggle for peasant rights.

Conscientization and Biblical Reflection

The work of conscientization within the MPP began by linking the Bible to social conditions. In the center we studied the Exodus story in the Bible, and I tried to compare the story of the people of Israel with the story of the people of Haiti.

Little by little I tried to understand the message of God who sent Moses to liberate the people of Israel, and what it meant for the people of Haiti. We looked at the reality of poverty, exploitation and injustice in Haiti in light of the Bible, and we asked what that meant for the lives of the peasants.

The experience in Papaye taught me that the Haitian people believe in God, but a different God than the one the Church was teaching. At that time the Haitian people had a traditional faith: they believed in saving their souls. Life in this world is not important, and the worse life is on earth the better it will be in heaven.

In contrast I saw the exploitation, repression by the paramilitary section chiefs and the army, economic speculation, and I felt that the situation must change. The catechism the people were receiving from the Church did not correspond to their reality. We tried to connect the message of the Bible to our social reality, to put "body" and "heart" together.

The principal work of the peasant movement is education, to open the eyes of the peasants so that they understand their reality. We use the example in the Bible where Jesus uses spittle to open the eyes of the blind. We try to open the eyes of the peasants so that they can see and change their reality.

Our work is oriented to action. We look at the problems of credit, land, technical assistance and marketing. We try to form cooperatives for storage and marketing. We also have activities related to the problems of illiteracy, of lack of potable water, and of human rights.

The strategy of the peasant movement today is to struggle and resist the coup and to demand democracy. Since the coup we have been forced by the military into hiding. We are trying to get out information on human rights abuses, and to work on small development projects for women.

Theology of Liberation in Haiti

The Haitian people believe in God, and we tried to help the people see the face of God each day. We cannot find salvation outside the struggle for liberation. God is present within our social reality. God accompanies us within this reality. The organizers within the MPP tried to bring this perspective to their parishes to change them.

We tried to help the peasants see that Jesus, who is the God of life, could not accept hunger, disease, exploitation, or death. For example, we would read the Gospel story of the multiplication of the loaves, or the account of the Last Supper. The Eucharist is the sacrament that celebrates our eating together at the same table.

We are one body in Christ. Within this body, we have different members, and each member has a role to play. Each member of the body is important; one is no more important than the other. When one member suffers, all the body suffers. The different members come together and share their goods in common. This looks like communism, but the church discovered this long before Marx.

In Haiti we have a Church of the Poor, the Church of Jesus Christ. The church of the rich is a church that has betrayed Jesus. The church is for the poor. The rich have a place on the condition that they agree to become poor. But Jesus came to liberate the poor. It's very clear in the Bible. The prophet Isaiah announced: "The Spirit of God is upon me to proclaim good news to the poor, to announce liberty to the oppressed, and to the hungry."

The Peasant Movement and President Aristide

I have worked with Father Aristide since 1986. Father Aristide worked in Port-au-Prince, and I worked in the rural areas helping the peasants to defend their rights. We both shared the same perspective of liberation theology. When the Macoutes attacked St. John Bosco parish on September 11, 1988, I was with Father Aristide in the church.

When Father Aristide was a candidate for President, he was the candidate of the Haitian people, of the Lavalas Party, and of the MPP. The relationship of MPP to Father Aristide is a close one, since we are both working for a new society. After the coup, the military tried to destroy the MPP, but they could not destroy the social consciousness of the people. To destroy the MPP you would have to destroy all the peasants.

The hope of the Papaye Peasant Movement has never changed. We want to change the situation of exploitation, repression, and oppression that exists in our country. We are in a permanent struggle for social change in Haiti, to build a society where each person can support his or her family, and everyone has life.

It's impossible to speak of democracy today without speaking about President Aristide's return. But the struggle goes far beyond that event. He is President for five years; freedom, however, is a constant struggle. The struggle for a new society will continue long after.

Ti Legliz: Haiti's 'Little Church' Movement And The Poor

by Mev Puleo

Many of Haiti's popular organizations trace their roots back to Haiti's Christian base community movement known as the Ti Kominite Legliz, *or "the Little Church." It was in these Christian base communities that activists found cover during the repressive Duvalier era to meet, reflect on their lives in light of their faith, and organize. The* Ti Legliz *movement provided a common thread that linked catechists, peasants, students and workers in a common struggle for justice. As could be expected, the Duvalier government persecuted these communities. Conflict also developed with the Church hierarchy, in large part due to Haiti's unique Concordat with the Vatican that allowed the Haitian government to appoint all of Haiti's bishops. This arrangement remained in place until it was revoked by John Paul II during his 1980s visit to Haiti.*

The following interviews with members of the Ti Legliz *in Haiti were conducted by Mev Puleo, a gifted author and photographer whose work on the Church and poor in Haiti has appeared in numerous magazines and books. This reflection appeared in the Fall 1993 edition of* Challenge, *EPICA's quarterly magazine.*

Traditionally, Catholic churches in Haiti were a place where old women and young children gathered in their best attire to attend Sunday Mass. Young people were scarcely visible, most of them either frequenting the more vibrant Pentecostal churches or abandoning church altogether. Beginning in the late 1970s, however, the emergence of the "little church" movement permanently changed this pattern of exodus.

These Christian base communities, known as *Ti Kominite Legliz* or *Ti Legliz* in Creole—the "little church community" or the "little church"—

161

seek to live out the preferential option for the poor, as articulated by the Conference of Latin American Bishops in Medellin in 1968, and reaffirmed at Puebla in 1979.

The "little church" movement grew in the 1970s and 1980s as a faith-based resistance to the Duvalier dictatorship, which fell in 1986. In December 1990 Father Jean-Bertrand Aristide, one of the priests working with the base communities, was elected President of Haiti. The secular and religious forces that opposed the base community movement from its birth again conspired to oppose and depose this "little priest" of the "little church," Father Jean-Bertrand Aristide. Since the September 1991 coup, the "little church" has been a prime target of repression from both the state and the Church hierarchy.

Members of Haiti's "little church" met with our delegation in a Haitian town in the fall of 1992. The one priest, two young men and two young women met with us at great risk, since meetings of more than two people are considered "suspect" by the military. The people sitting before us had seen their fellow community members arrested, disappeared and killed, and they know that the same fate may await them. Their names have been changed to protect their identities.

Father Emile: Since the coup, we are especially engaged in serving the people who are victims of the coup, giving reports of repression to human rights committees and to the media. Ours is a church of service. A church of solidarity with the poor. We are following the example and commitment of Christ, our older brother. It is an "evangelical engagement,"—a wholehearted commitment, a marriage of theory and practice. This is how we came to have problems with certain authorities within the church and with other high-placed people.

Veronique: Our vision is to arrive at the Kingdom of God on earth—where everybody can find a place to live, everybody can find food, everyone can find a way to stay alive. Many of us will die as we work for this, but others will remain to continue the work. We are struggling with the poor to arrive at a just society. We find community within the poor neighborhoods.

The strategy of the "little church" today is a Biblical strategy, an evangelical strategy. We want to appear to the people as salt in the food, so we can give the masses, the Christian community, hope. We want people to see that there is a light in their midst, a light in the darkness.

In spite of the difficulties we face, the "little church" may become diminished, but it will never be crushed because we are not only working with the power of our own minds and hands, but with the power of the Holy Spirit.

One Foot in Faith, One Foot in Reality

André: In our early years, from about 1980 to 1984, the institutional church was with us, but maybe that's because it didn't think we would actually embrace the notion of the option for the poor. But when Jean Claude Duvalier's dictatorship became really ferocious, and the *Tontons Macoutes* (Duvalier's police force) were crushing the people with heavy repression, we became more firm in our option for the poor, which for us meant organizing the poor.

Even though the church hierarchy was fairly united against the Duvalier regime by the mid 1980s, it still began to see us as a problematic element within the church. When Jean-Claude Duvalier left, they started labeling us "subversives"—in Creole they called the "little church" the "little local communists."

They even brainwashed the Catholic radio station, Radio Soleil, against us, so it stopped responding to our press releases. This process of defamation and brainwashing, as well as the repression directed against us, has gotten worse since the coup.

Today we are in the second stage of the "little church." Despite everything, the "little church" is still standing. Our work continues, especially organizing people in the popular or poor neighborhoods. We let people know that they cannot stand only on one foot. The Word of God teaches us that for a person to be really human, he or she has to stand on the foot of faith and also on the foot of the reality which we are living.

God is with the Poor

Raymond: This is our problem with the "big church." They gave us God upstairs. But we know that God is One who lives among the poor. This is the theological position of the "little church"—the theology of liberation.

In the "little church" we don't only share the word with the people, but we share everything we have with the people. If we buy a piece of sugar cane, we cut it into little pieces and share it. Any kind of food we share with each other to show the people that sharing is not only sharing words, but sharing of your life—you have to eat, too!

You see, the "little church" offers a challenge to the "big church." The priest can say, "Go with the peace of Christ." Then, one person goes to eat at his or her house, but another person has nothing to eat at home. This is not peace! When one goes away full and another empty handed, there is no peace. This is why we are struggling, to change the church so that it doesn't participate in this kind of injustice anymore.

André: We in the "little church" community are like family. These people sitting next to me are more my brothers and sisters than my immediate family who live with me at home. When we meet as sisters and brothers in the church, we feel much closer than we do with our families.

In the church, if one doesn't have money, but the other has money—we share! If my sister has money, I have money! For example, if I have to travel into the countryside, I can ask any "little church" member and they will share money for my travels—without any conditions or strings attached.

Raymond: And, in this case, it is the poor sharing with the poor. All the people of the "little church" are unemployed or underemployed. Those who do work only make about $2 a day—this is just a disguise for unemployment. This economic struggle to survive weakens us.

In the Gospel of Luke, Jesus says, "The Spirit of God is upon me, and God has sent me to announce the good news to the poor." That good news is sight, liberation, freedom. We think that if we are good news to the poor, we are bad news to the rich.

Women and the Church

Marie: In the "little church," women do the same work as the men. If there are men coordinators, there are also women coordinators. The men interpret the Bible, and so do the women. We also work with the people. And we participate in and support women's organizations in the neighborhoods.

In other words, women have their role in the society and within the church, and the men working in the "little church" know that we are the same as they are. We are sisters and brothers. There is no superior, no inferior. We are like finger and ring.

But look at the work we began to undertake in the church of St. John Bosco, Aristide's parish. We started to have altar girls and we had an open mike where we let the poor speak. It became a church of sharing, where not only the priest was preaching. I think it was for that reason that the church of St. John Bosco was burned down in September 1988 as Father Aristide was saying Mass.

Tontons Macoutes stormed the church, attacking people with rocks, guns, knives, and picks. Seventeen people were killed, 77 wounded and the church was burned to the ground as the army watched. One of our organizers was murdered by the thugs. They hacked him to pieces with a machete right inside the church.

The Question of Violence and Nonviolence

Raymond: In the movement at this time, we are fighting by peaceful means. But we have to defend our lives and our very existence. Life is something very important! Jesus accepted giving up his live to give life to other people. Jesus doesn't accept death at all!

But let's take an example. From September 29, 1991 until the present, about 4,000 people have been killed. Does Jesus accept the death of those 4,000 people who died with empty hands? But if those people had had something in their hands with which to defend themselves, some of them wouldn't be dead and some of their attackers would have died.

Today in Haiti, even if you are sitting peacefully at home, they can come for you with pistols and kill you. Will Jesus tell you to throw up your arms and let someone kill you? Legitimate self-defense is a right.

There are many examples—the Farabundo Marti National Liberation Front in El Salvador, the Sandinista Front in Nicaragua, and other groups have organized themselves for change. Their right to self-defense enabled them to resist the US government and the repressive governments in their home countries.

André: For those of us who choose nonviolence, it doesn't mean that we are going to make compromises. Nonviolence is a nonviolent struggle for truth, justice, love and the dignity of every person. The institutional church criticizes us for supporting "violence." This is not true. We are not violent, but we desire to follow in Christ's footsteps, imitating Jesus who doesn't accept compromise.

Father Emile: I think it is really important for us to sit down with groups like yours. We are all working together for creative change. This is not just a dialogue, but a sharing of life. We must tell you, though, that even as we are alive right here before your eyes, we could also die. We never know who is watching us, but we know that the enemy has spies.

We invite you to deepen your own work so that we will be closer to having democracy and justice in all the Americas. As long as this work is not carried on, day to day, it is the poor who suffer. And the anger of the poor is growing more and more. If things do not turn around, the people will explode and that explosion will cause more harm than good. If there is a revolution, many, many people will perish.

Cuba and Religion: From The Revolution To John Paul II

by María López Vigil

It has been said that when the Cuban revolution triumphed in 1959, 95 percent of Cubans were revolutionaries; they supported what had happened. And 95 percent were religious; they believed in a "superior" being. At that time, Cuban religiosity was a complex mixture of traditional Catholicism and Santería—the animistic religion of the uprooted African slaves. The Second Vatican Council had not yet occurred. Indigenous religiosity did not form part of this original mixture; the years of the conquest had brutally eliminated Cuba's native peoples. The relation between Church and State during the first 20 years of the revolution pointed to conflict, tension and a lack of understanding. Things changed in the 1980s with the National Gathering of Cuban Churches (ENEC) and the publication of Fray Betto's book, Fidel and Religion. *The fall of the Berlin Wall, the collapse of the Soviet Union and state socialism in Eastern Europe, and the disappearance of nearly 80 percent of Cuba's trade further accelerated changes that paved the way for the historic visit of John Paul II to Cuba in January 1998.*
The following article provides a glimpse into the recent history of the relationship between the Cuban government and the Churches. Written by María López Vigil, it appeared in the December 1997 edition of Envío Magazine, *published by the Central American University (UCA) in Nicaragua.*

"It would be an error to believe that everything happened because we became Marxists, when the truth is that we became Marxists because of everything that happened," remembers a truly Marxist Cuban, evoking the humanist nature that characterized the Cuban revolution from the very first moment. This social justice project is the basis of the consensus and massive support that has sustained the revolution for so many years and through so many difficulties, the greatest of all being the arrogance of the United States.

The social achievements in Cuba, creating wealth and redistributing it more justly, massifying participation, dignity, education at all levels, work, preventive and curative health, culture, sports, social security, in short, "everything that happened," made the deficits in the way the revolution treated popular religiosity much less significant. The concern for humankind, responsibility for the common good and caring for life are gifts of gold in all great religions.

Love for others is the verifying test in the Christian faith. Christian faith is either love or it doesn't exist. In the 1970s, Latin America, the only continent that is both majority impoverished and majority Christian, witnessed the birth and development of liberation theology and base communities. That development contributed to fruitful alliances between Christians and revolutionaries and, above all, saw the blood of believers—pastors, priests, nuns, catechists, even bishops—shed in the name of the struggle "against atheistic communism" by the US government and its allies, the Latin American dictatorships.

What happened in Cuba in those years remains a painful enigma: a state concerned with social justice and sovereign dignity, but one that marginalized churches, undervalued religion and promoted atheism. Some Christian churches were paralyzed, silenced, keeping their distance from this state that promoted justice and sovereignty, not knowing how to dialogue with it.

When Fidel spoke in Chile in 1972 and in Jamaica in 1977 to Christians who supported the social transformation processes happening in those countries, and when he applauded the "strategic alliance" between Christians and Marxists, the religious in Cuba saw that message as a revolutionary product "for export."

Two events in 1979 began to shake up the conflict between the state and religion. This movement came maybe late and certainly slowly, as slowly as most things move in Cuba. But the hour arrived. In January of that year, the meeting of the Catholic bishops in Puebla "touched" the Cuban Catholic Church and woke it up. And the July triumph of the Sandinista revolution in Nicaragua moved Cuba, the continent and the world.

The National Gathering of Cuban Churches

Various Cuban bishops attended the Puebla meeting, but their peculiar perspective was barely noted in its final documents. In those years Latin American reality was very homogenous and overwhelming. Cuba and its Church lived such a different reality that the country's religious, such an obvious minority, did not manage either to define anything or to communicate adequately after so many years of self-absorption.

Recognizing this gap and trying to fill it, seeking responses to questions of what the Cuban Church says about itself and what it can say to the other Churches, having "a Puebla in Cuba" led in 1979 to the National Gathering of Cuban Churches (ENEC). The years preparing for this event, which took place in 1986, revitalized the Cuban Church, its hierarchy and its bases. It also contributed to the Church community finding out more about what was happening outside of the "walls" of the paralyzed Cuban Church.

ENEC shook the floor of the Catholic Church, its hierarchy and its minority but united bases. It was a stellar moment. Preparing for ENEC demanded five years of surveys, studies and research meetings, debates, retreats and get-togethers, and parish, vicariate and diocesan assemblies. It demanded a serene look at the past and a daring look at the future.

Even though discrimination against religious people began to lose strength in the mid-1980s—among other reasons because education, even though atheistic, educated everyone—the wounds were still unhealed. One of the toughest issues for the Catholic authorities and grassroots to assimilate was that of dialogue and reconciliation with the government. It was the issue that met with the most resistance. "We were distrustful because of everything that had happened. We feared dialogue, not because we were persecuted, but because we feared being manipulated," explains one Catholic.

Despite everything, ENEC fulfilled its mission of opening spaces. "All of us who experienced it took away from it the experience of having a living church, with more spaces for participation, with open debate," it was explained to me. "We lay people felt listened to. We witnessed a change of mentalities." When I hear people speak today so enthusiastically about that experience, it seems to me that ENEC was for Cuban Catholics a concentration of three events that the other Latin American Churches had lived much earlier and in stages: Vatican II, Medellin and Puebla.

Nicaragua's Gift to Cuba

What was happening, meanwhile, in the official arena? There had been a halting distension between the government and the ecclesiastical authorities: facilities for reconstructing abandoned churches or for religious personnel to acquire vehicles for their work, official support for nuns who worked in homes for the elderly or other "charity works," etc. Although there was more latitude and tolerance, however, being religious remained a sort of negative social mark and official discrimination continued.

The great shift in the Cuban revolution's perception of religion would come through Nicaragua's revolution. After 20 years of fruitlessly supporting guerrilla groups who fought to take power throughout the continent, the now mature Cuban revolutionary process witnessed the birth of a little sister only a two-hour flight from home.

Cubans by the thousands flocked to Nicaragua: doctors, teachers, technicians, military inspectors, sports trainers. There was massive collaboration in all fields. And thousands of Nicaraguans went to Cuba on scholarships to study; others, especially those with war disabilities, went to get medical treatment; others went to politically sightsee, or just went on vacation—but always to learn. In this ongoing daily interchange that lasted over ten years, Cubans witnessed that the religiosity of a good part of the Nicaraguan people was not in contradiction with the revolution. They discovered that, apart from the political conflict between various church authorities and the Nicaraguan government, there was "something else" in Nicaraguans' culture of rebellion and in the mortar of Sandinismo.

They found priests who were both ministers of God and ministers of the people. They experienced liberation theology not "in opposition" and denouncing injustice, as in the rest of Latin America, but "in power" and announcing achievements. This only happened in Sandino's Nicaragua. They discovered something of the harvest that had been achieved after a long period of sowing authentic Christian values fertilized with so much blood. Cubans in Nicaragua also saw a similar and even more relevant reality in El Salvador—those were the glorious years of Monsignor Romero—and in Guatemala, with its unending martyrdom.

Feeling its way, Cuba peeked at a hidden face of the religious "phenomenon." I still remember how a Managua Christian base community recoiled at this word. A Cuban functionary, scientific atheist and "expert in religious issues," came to the community and introduced himself. He had come, he said, to observe the "religious phenomenon." An upstart, irreverent woman stood up in pure Nica fashion and faced him: "Look, we're no two-headed goat, we are not a phenomenon!"

Tripping over each other, hundreds of Communist functionaries from the Cuban government, together with thousands of Cubans who collaborated with the Sandinista revolution with exemplary generosity, gave up in the face of the evidence that it was not just a phenomenon to be studied in books or congresses, but a warm and living questioning of Cuba's frozen reality. It was perhaps the greatest contribution little Nicaragua made to its older sister in those years.

Fidel and Religion: A Bolt of Lightning

Cubans weren't the only ones who came to see and admire the Nicaraguan "phenomenon." In the 1980s Nicaragua became the destination of all the nonconformists on the planet: an open plaza, a Mecca or door to Bethlehem that people visited, pulled by its star or obliged by their faith. And those visitors always questioned the veracity of the slogan, "There is no contradiction between Christianity and revolution."

One such visitor, who went from Havana to Managua and from there returned to Brazil only to come back again to Cuba and Nicaragua, hit the mark in history. The impassioned lucidity of Brazilian Dominican Fray Betto contributed significantly to the religious thaw in Cuba.

In May 1985, Betto interviewed Fidel Castro for 23 hours, focusing on an issue untouched in hundreds of previous interviews: Fidel and religion. That's what he called the book that covers that historical conversation. It came out in Cuba at the end of 1985, and its thousands of copies sold out in hours. It has been one of the greatest best-sellers in Cuba.

The title of the book alone was a novelty and a provocation after 26 years of conflicts and run-ins. More and more copies were sold. The Cuban population devoured its 379 pages. And without yet digesting those pages, people began to comment ardently on what they had read. Seen from without, nothing was exactly shocking, in either form or content, although the text did contain some totally unknown biographical information and anecdotes about Fidel.

Since there were neither revelations nor exclusives, what caused such upheaval on the island? It was the respect, the civility, and above all the appreciation with which Fidel spoke—for the first time—so extensively of "religion," especially Christianity, and more specifically Catholicism, which is what he knows best, since he was educated in that religion for 12 years and its authorities were at the origin of the conflicts.

There was no lack of reticence and distancing by some ecclesiastical authorities, but "the religious" people received the book and what it announced with happiness. Among Cuban communists—especially among the fanatics, mid-level functionaries and those coldest toward religious issues—feelings sizzled. Many began to move from suspicion toward rejection. "It was like a bolt of lightning hit official ideology," remembers a friend of mine.

In those same months, Cuba invited the Latin American heads of state to an event to discuss the continent's unpayable foreign debt and a group of us Latin American Christians had a public pulpit in Havana with a warm welcome. In those same months Fidel appeared at the pulpit of the Methodist Church in Vedado, with his hand on the Bible, accompanying US minister Jesse Jackson in a religious service. "There can't be anything wrong with religion when Fidel pays so much attention to it," was the general reflection on those events.

Signs began to appear on all sides. But the positions that crystallize in times of conflict are the most difficult to modify. And Cuban "atheism" was in large measure, the crystallization of a political crisis that, though rusty, was still present. It was hard for Cuban atheists to stop being dogmatic, judgmental atheists, especially in those years when the Cuban revolution continued its inexorable march and little Cuba was confidently moving forward, resources were overflowing and optimism predominated in society.

In those final "normal" years, before the Cuban government inaugurated the "special period" at the end of 1990, there was talk on various occasions of a possible visit by John Paul II to Cuba as another sign of the opening and of new times in Church-State relations. There were ups and downs, fears and expectations between the Catholic and government authorities, still distrusting and testing each other. Finally, the crisis began to justify putting off the event year after year, sometimes for one reason and sometimes for another, waiting for the most propitious moment.

1991: Party Doors Are Opened

The Cuban Communist Party lived its stellar moment with the preparation of the Fourth Congress in 1990. Six hundred thousand Cuban Communists were called to debate a brave, self-critical text, "The Call." It called on everyone's creativity to respond to the new situation that the island was beginning to experience after the fall of European socialism. Among the issues to be debated for the Fourth Congress were the elimination from the Cuban Communist Party statutes of the discrimination established 25 years earlier that prohibited believers from joining the party.

Although the time now seemed to be ripe, it was still not easy. The antireligious defenses taught in school, inculcated in the party nucleus, present in official propaganda, turned out still to be quite active. "Eliminating this discrimination was the most heatedly debated motion, the one that faced the most resistance and had the least consensus," a militant told me years later.

Finally, in the name of national unity, the Cuban Communist Party opened its doors to believers in its Fourth Congress (October 1991), conserving in its definition the same Marxist-Leninist identity and therefore a determined materialist philosophy. The opinion that Fidel had expressed to Fray Betto in his book—and insisted on in debates in Congress with all the weight of his authority—was decisive.

A Communist militant pointed out to me that the Cuban Communist Party has never made public the number of believers who joined the party after the 1991 opening. "Probably because there weren't very many," he said, then added: "More than believers joining the party, what happened is that many militants confessed their beliefs, and many of them their belief in Santería. I think the main effect of the measure was that the party became more honest with itself."

The next year, 1992, with the reforms to the 1976 Constitution, the government took a much more transcendental step, though one less publicized and barely reflected on. All explicit or implicit expressions that committed the revolutionary state to atheism were eliminated from the constitutional text. The Cuban state began finally to be a secular state. But by then the material and spiritual, the objective and subjective signs of the Cuban crisis were painfully obvious and a new space opened up for religiosity. The religious faithful also began to develop a new agenda.

Fidel Castro And John Paul II: An Encounter In Cuba

Discourse of Fidel Castro

The visit of John Paul II to Cuba and his meeting with Fidel Castro has been a historic event that would have been inconceivable only a few years ago. Such a meeting did not occur by happenstance. It was well-prepared, both in terms of the depth of the problems that it addressed—expressed by John Paul II with absolute freedom and heard by Fidel Castro with absolute normality—as well as in terms of the external preparations such as the Eucharists, the impressive choral displays, the participation of the multitudes, etc. Nevertheless, it took 40 years for this event to occur. The central actors, John Paul II and Fidel Castro, both display charismatic personalities and firm convictions. But it was the dynamics of history that brought about the encounter.
The following discourse was delivered by Cuban President Fidel Castro in January 1998, upon the arrival of John Paul II to the airport in Havana.

Your Holiness:

The ground that you just kissed is honored by your presence. You will not find here those peaceful and generous native inhabitants who populated this land when the first Europeans arrived on this island. Almost all of them were exterminated by the exploitation and slave labor that they could not resist; the women were converted into objects of pleasure or domestic servants, and the men were killed beneath the swords or victims of unknown diseases that the conquistadors brought with them. Some priests left the wrenching witness of their protest against such crimes.

Over the centuries, more than a million Africans were cruelly uprooted from their distant lands and replaced the Indian slaves who had been exterminated. They made a profound contribution to the ethnic composition and the origins of the people who currently populate our country, where culture, beliefs and the blood of everyone participated in this dramatic history. The conquest and the colonization of the entire hemisphere is estimated to have cost the lives of 70 million Indians and the enslavement of millions of Africans. Much blood was spilled and many injustices were committed, the great part of them under other forms of exploitation after centuries of sacrifices and struggles that continue today.

Cuba, under extremely difficult conditions, was able to build a nation. It struggled with insuperable heroism to achieve its independence. Exactly 100 years ago it suffered a real holocaust in the concentration camps where a considerable part of the population died, particularly women, elderly and children. The crime of the colonialists, which will never be forgotten in the conscience of humanity, was barbaric. You, child of Poland and witness to Auschwitz, can understand this better than anyone.

Today, Your Holiness, we are faced with genocide, through hunger, disease, and a total economic asphyxiation of a people who refuses to submit itself to the dictates of an empire of the most economically, politically and militarily powerful nation in history. Much more powerful than ancient Rome, which for centuries forced those who refused to renounce their faith to be devoured by wild beasts. Like those Christians who were atrociously slandered by those who sought to justify their crimes, we are slandered like them, and would prefer to die 100 times rather than renounce our convictions. Like the Church, the revolution also has many martyrs.

Your Holiness, we have the same thoughts that you have about many important questions in the world today, and that gives us great satisfaction. In other matters, our opinions differ, but we render great respect to you for the profound conviction with which you defend your ideas.

In the long pilgrimage for the world you have been able to see with your own eyes much injustice, inequality, poverty; lands that are not cultivated and peasants without food and land; unemployment, hunger, disease; lives that could be saved with a few cents but perish; illiteracy, child prostitution, six-year-old children working or begging in order to live; marginalized neighborhoods where hundreds of millions of people live in subhuman conditions; discrimination on account of race and sex; whole ethnic groups displaced from their lands and abandoned to fate; fear of strangers, disrespect toward other peoples, cultures destroyed; underdevelopment, usurious loans, unpayable debts; unequal trade relations, unproductive financial speculation; the environment mercilessly destroyed and perhaps without remedy;

unscrupulous sale of arms with repugnant aims of profit; wars, violence, massacres, generalized corruption, drugs, vice and alienating consumerism that is imposed as the idyllic model on all peoples.

Humanity has grown, just in this century, almost four times. There are thousands of millions who suffer hunger and thirst for justice. The list of economic and social calamities of humankind is interminable. I know that these are things that are of a permanent and growing concern of Your Holiness.

I have had personal experiences that permit me to appreciate other aspects of your thinking. I attended Catholic schools up to the time of my graduation. I was taught that to be a Protestant, a Jew, a Muslim, a Buddhist, an animist, or a participant in other religious beliefs constituted a horrible sin, deserving of the most severe and implacable punishment. More than once—even in those schools for the rich and privileged that I attended—it occurred to me to ask why there weren't Black children there, and I have not forgotten the unconvincing answers that I received. Years later, the Second Vatican Council, called together by Pope John XXIII, addressed many of these delicate questions.

We are aware of the efforts that Your Holiness has made to preach and to practice these sentiments of respect toward believers of other important and influential religions that extend throughout the world. The respect toward believers and nonbelievers is a basic principle that Cuban revolutionaries have stubbornly passed on to our compatriots. This principles have been defined and guaranteed by our Constitution and by our laws. If difficulties have occasionally arisen, it has never been the fault of the revolution. We harbor the hope that one day no schoolchild, anywhere in the world, will ever have to ask why there are no Black, Indian, Asian or White children in the school.

Your Holiness, I sincerely admire your valiant declarations about what happened to Galileo, the errors of the Inquisition, the bloody episodes of the Crusades, the crimes committed during the conquest of America, and other scientists whose discoveries nobody questions today, but who in their time were the victim of prejudice and anathemas. All these matters required the immense authority that you have acquired in the Church to be addressed adequately.

What can we offer you in Cuba, Your Holiness? A people with less inequality, fewer citizens without any support, fewer children without schools, fewer sick people without hospitals, more teachers and more doctors per inhabitant than any other country in the world that Your Holiness has visited. An educated people to whom you may speak with as much liberty as you choose, with complete security; a people of talent, with political awareness, profound convictions, absolute confidence in their ideas, with a conscience and all the respect in the world to hear you.

There is no country better prepared to understand your ideas, as we understand them, nor so alike in mind as that which you preach to us concerning equal distribution of wealth, and the solidarity between men and women and all peoples that should be globalized.

Welcome to Cuba!

Homily of John Paul II

Both the Cuban government and the Cuban Churches have changed profoundly since the triumph of the Cuban revolution in 1959. In 1986, the National Gathering of Cuban Churches (ENEC) analyzed the national and church situation and recognized the values of the revolution and socialist society, seeing in them the action of God, although this did not take away the tension. In a reciprocal fashion, Fidel Castro began to express his admiration for liberation theology and committed Christians who gave their life for justice. While tensions continue, these fundamental changes in the thinking of the Churches and the State laid the foundation for the historic encounter between Fidel Castro and John Paul II.

The following homily was delivered by John Paul II at Mass in Havana's Plaza of the Revolution on January 25, 1998 during his historic visit to Cuba. In it, John Paul presented a strong defense of social justice, freedom and solidarity, and offered a sharp critique of neoliberalism for subordinating the human person "to blind market forces," and placing "unbearable burdens upon less favored countries." Fidel Castro, seated with the congregation and not on the liturgical podium, waited for the Pope to descend after Mass and shook his hand and the hands of the Cuban bishops.

"This day is holy to the Lord your God; do not mourn or weep" (Nehemiah 8:9). With great joy I celebrate Holy Mass in this Square of José Martí, on Sunday, the Lord's Day, which should be dedicated to rest, prayer and family life. The Word of God calls us together to grow in faith and to celebrate the presence of the Risen Lord in our midst, for "by one Spirit we were all baptized into one body" (1 Corinthians 12:13), the Mystical Body of Christ that is the Church. Jesus Christ unites all the baptized. From him flows the fraternal love among Cuban Catholics and Catholics everywhere, since all are "the body of Christ and individually members of it" (1 Corinthians 12:27). The Church in Cuba is not alone or isolated; rather, it is part of the Universal Church that extends throughout the whole world.

With affection I greet Cardinal Jaime Ortega, the Pastor of this Archdiocese, and I thank him for his kind words at the beginning of this celebration, telling me of the joys and the hopes that mark the life of this ecclesial community. I likewise greet the Cardinals present from different countries, my Brother Bishops in Cuba, and the Bishops from other places who have wished to take part in this solemn celebration. I cordially greet the priests, the men and women religious and all the faithful assembled here in such numbers. I assure each one of you of my affection and closeness in the Lord.

I also thank the civil authorities who have wished to be present today and I am grateful for the cooperation that they have provided.

"The Spirit of the Lord is upon me, because he has anointed me to preach good news to the poor" (Luke 4:18). Every minister of God has to make his own these words spoken by Jesus in Nazareth. And so, as I come among you, I wish to bring you the Good News of hope in God. As a servant of the Gospel I bring you this message of love and solidarity that Jesus Christ, by his coming, offers to men and women in every age. In absolutely no way is this an ideology or a new economic or political system; rather, it is a path of authentic peace, justice and freedom.

The ideological and economic systems succeeding one another in the last two centuries have often encouraged conflict as a method since their programs contained the seeds of opposition and disunity. This fact profoundly affected their understanding of the human person and of its relations with others. Some of these systems also presumed to relegate religion to the merely private sphere, stripping it of any social influence or importance. In this regard, it is helpful to recall that a modern State cannot make atheism or religion one of its political ordinances. The State, while distancing itself from all extremes of fanaticism or secularism, should encourage a harmonious social climate and suitable legislation that enables every person and every religious confession to live their faith freely, to express that faith in public life and to count on adequate resources and opportunities to bring its spiritual, moral and civic benefits to bear on the life of the nation.

On the other hand, various places are witnessing the resurgence of a certain capitalist neoliberalism that subordinates the human person to blind market forces and conditions the development of peoples on those forces. From its centers of power, such neoliberalism often places unbearable burdens upon less favored countries. Hence, at times, unsustainable economic programs are imposed on nations as a condition for further assistance. In the international community, we thus see a small number of countries growing exceedingly rich at the cost of the increasing impoverishment of a great number of other countries; as a result the wealthy grow ever wealthier, while the poor grow ever poorer.

Dear brothers and sisters: the Church is a teacher in humanity. Faced with these systems, she presents a culture of love and of life, restoring hope to humanity, hope in the transforming power of love lived in the unity willed by Christ. For this to happen, it is necessary to follow a path of reconciliation, dialogue and fraternal acceptance of one's neighbor, of every human person.

The Church, in carrying out her mission, sets before the world a new justice, the justice of the Kingdom of God (Matthew 6:33). On various occasions I have spoken on social themes. It is necessary to keep speaking on these themes, as long as any injustice, however small, is present in the world; otherwise the Church would not be faithful to the mission entrusted to her by Christ. At stake here is the concrete human person. While times and situations may change, there are always people who need the voice of the Church so that their difficulties, their suffering and their distress may be known. Those who find themselves in these situations can be certain that they will not be betrayed, for the Church is with them and the Pope, in his heart and with his words of encouragement, embraces all who suffer injustice.

On the threshold of the year 2000, the teachings of Jesus maintain their full force. They are valid for all of you, dear brothers and sisters. In seeking the justice of the Kingdom we cannot hesitate in the face of difficulties and misunderstandings. If the Master's call to justice, to service and to love is accepted as good news, then the heart is expanded, criteria are transformed and a culture of love and life is born. This is the great change that society needs and expects; and it can only come about if there is first a conversion of each individual heart, as a condition for the necessary changes in the structures of society.

"The Spirit of the Lord has sent me to proclaim release to the captives, to set at liberty those who are oppressed" (Luke 4:18). The good news of Jesus must be accompanied by a proclamation of freedom based on the solid foundation of truth: "If you continue in my word, you are truly my disciples, and you will know the truth and the truth will make you free" (John 8:31-32). The truth of which Jesus speaks is not only the intellectual grasp of reality, but also the truth about the human person and its transcendent condition, its rights and duties, its greatness and its limitations. It is the same truth that Jesus proclaimed with his life, reaffirmed before Pilate and, by his silence, before Herod; it is the same truth that led him to his saving Cross and his glorious Resurrection.

A freedom that is not based on truth conditions the human person in such a way that it sometimes becomes the object and not the subject of its social, cultural, economic and political surroundings; this leaves it almost no initiative for its personal development. At other times that freedom takes on an individualistic cast and, with no regard for the freedom of others, imprisons the human person in its own egoism. The attainment of freedom in responsibility is a duty that no one can shirk. For Christians, the freedom of the children of God is not only a gift and a task, but its attainment also involves an invaluable witness and a genuine contribution to the journey toward the liberation of the whole human race. This liberation cannot be reduced to its social and political aspects, but rather reaches its fullness in the exercise of freedom of conscience, the basis and foundation of all other human rights.

For many of the political and economic systems operative today the greatest challenge is still that of combining freedom and social justice, freedom and solidarity, so that no one is relegated to a position of inferiority. The Church's social doctrine is meant to be a reflection and a contribution that can shed light on and reconcile the relationship between the inalienable rights of each individual and the needs of society, so that people can attain their profound aspirations and integral fulfillment in accordance with their conditions as sons and daughters of God and citizens in society. Hence the Catholic laity should contribute to this fulfillment by the application of the Church's social teachings in every sector open to people of good will.

In the Gospel proclaimed today, justice is seen as intimately linked to truth. This is also evident in the enlightened thinking of the Fathers of your Country. The Servant of God, Father Felix Varela, inspired by his Christian faith and his fidelity to the priestly ministry, sowed in the heart of the Cuban people the seeds of justice and freedom that he dreamed of seeing blossom in an independent Cuba.

The teaching of José Martí on love between all people had profoundly evangelical roots, and thus overcame the false conflict between faith in God and love and service to one's country. This great leader wrote: "Pure, selfless, persecuted, tormented, poetic and simple, the religion of the Nazarene enthralled all honorable persons.... Every people needs to be religious. Not only as part of its essence, but for its own practical benefit it needs to be religious.... An irreligious people will die, because nothing in it encourages virtue. Human injustices offend virtue; it is necessary that heavenly justice guarantee it."

As everyone knows, Cuba has a Christian soul and this has brought her a universal vocation. Called to overcome isolation, she needs to open herself to the world and the world needs to draw close to Cuba, her people, her sons and daughters who are surely her greatest wealth. This is the time to start out on the new paths called for by the times of renewal that we are experiencing at the approach of the Third Millennium of the Christian era!

We Make the Road By Walking

Dear brothers and sisters: God has blessed this people with true educators of the national conscience, clear and firm models of the Christian faith as the most effective support of virtue and love. Today the Bishops, with the priests, men and women religious and lay faithful, are striving to build bridges in order to bring minds and hearts closer together; they are fostering and strengthening peace, and preparing the civilization of love and justice. I am present among you as a messenger of truth and hope. For this reason I wish to repeat my appeal: let Jesus Christ enlighten you; accept without reservation the splendor of his truth, so that all can set out on the path of unity through love and solidarity, while avoiding exclusion, isolation and conflict, which are contrary to the will of God who is Love.

May the Holy Spirit enlighten by his gifts those who, in different ways, are responsible for the future of this people so close to my heart. And may our Lady of Charity of El Cobre, Queen of Cuba, obtain for her children the gifts of peace, progress and happiness.

VII

The Witness
Of The
Martyrs

The Gospel In El Quiché: The Blood Of The Martyrs

by Juan Ixchop

One of the most impressive and dramatic fruits of the past three decades in Central America, Mexico and the Caribbean, is the witness of the martyrs. Traditionally, martyrs are those who gave witness to their faith, even to the point of death. Since the Second Vatican Council, however, bearing witness to one's faith and working for social justice have become more intimately linked.

Perhaps more than any other country, Guatemala has produced the most martyrs. As in El Salvador, hundreds of catechists, dozens of women religious and priests have been assassinated for their faith and commitment to justice. Most recently, Bishop Juan Gerardi, director of the Recovery of the Historic Memory (REMHI) project, was brutally assassinated. In Guatemala, however, entire communities of indigenous Christians have been massacred and offered the ultimate witness of their faith. Their witness makes real the ancient wisdom of the Church: "The blood of the martyrs is the seed of new Christians."

In the following interview, Juan Ixchop narrates the dramatic story of his community in El Quiché. He is an indigenous catechist and a member of the formation team of a network of Christian base communities. His story appeared in the Summer 1993 edition of Challenge, *EPICA's quarterly magazine.*

The day my father was killed, he had set out early in the morning with his horse and a load of firewood he wanted to sell in the market. When he returned from the market in the afternoon, the army killed him, along with 31 others. Before killing my father, the army tortured him, cutting off his hand and then his head. They blew out the brains of some of the people, and cut up the bodies of others into smaller pieces like firewood.

Before my father was killed, he told us, "Dear children, dear wife, never abandon your Christian faith. Never forget the community. Go forward, cultivate the little land that we have so that you have food next year. You children will be left with your mother. You, my wife, will be left with these children. You will suffer many more sad and painful things, but I am going away." Then my father added, "If I am left for dead in the village or by the side of the road, don't risk your lives to bury me."

We weren't able to bury my father. My father's body, and the bodies of the other 31 people, were eaten by the vultures. The army said if we buried the cadavers we would die in the same way. This happened on July 22, 1981. The army justified the massacre saying that the people killed were bad people, who were promoting the community to organize and demand their rights.

My father was a catechist, and a member of the Committee of Peasant Unity (CUC), which demanded just wages for farm workers. For years the Catholic Church had been working to empower people in the community to work for our own development. The Church had discovered the sufferings of our people and committed itself to help. First Bible reflection groups were organized, then groups of catechists, and finally a community improvement association. This committee worked to build a school, repair the roads, and introduce potable water into the community.

The army continued to persecute and massacre our community. They wanted to kill my whole family. I had two older brothers. One day the army surrounded our house and broke down the door. They didn't find us there because we had already fled and were hiding in the mountains, sleeping beneath some trees. The army put all of our clothing in one pile inside the house and set fire to everything. They burned our corn, so we wouldn't have anything to eat. Then they burned down the neighbors' houses too.

The army captured one man who stayed behind, and carved out his intestines. They grabbed another man who was returning from an evangelical cult with his Bible in hand. He didn't flee because he believed if the army captured him and killed him, it would be the will of God. That's how the repression began.

The Martyrdom of Six Catechists

By the time General Rios Montt took power, during a military coup on March 22, 1982, the rest of the people in my village joined us in the mountains to save their lives. For seven months, until October, we hid in the mountains until we couldn't bear the persecution any longer.

So we named representatives of our community to go and speak to the army at their command post in Santa Cruz Quiché. We were ready to risk death, if necessary, but we couldn't go on anymore hiding in the mountains.

We told the army to stop killing us, we were ready to accept the civil defense patrols (PACs) in our community.

The army was jubilant. "Finally, you've come back. We're not going to kill you. We'll go back with you to the community and meet with everyone, so we can form the civil patrols." We thought that the army would stop killing us.

But then the army came to our community. They kidnapped six people and tortured them for 15 days in the military barracks. Then they came back to our community and turned the people over to us saying, "These are bad people, they're inciting you to organize and demand your rights. We're coming back in a week. If you don't kill them yourselves, all of you will die."

"What are we going to do?" people asked. "If we don't kill you the whole community will be killed. But how can we kill you?" The six men replied, "If you have to kill us, we know it isn't your will but an order of the army. We will save you. We are prepared to give up our lives."

Some of the men were our relatives. They were different ages, from 25 to 40 years old. Their names were Pedro Castro, Gustavo Castro, Jesús López, Emilio Segundo, Santos Chivalán, and Agustin Chivalán. They were members of the Committee of Peasant Unity (CUC). They were also catechists, and had been active in Catholic Action. One of the six was a Mayan priest.

If You Want to Die, Keep Organizing

At the end of the week the army came back and took the six men to the cemetery with the rest of our community. Then the army forced the community to kill the six men. I couldn't bear to look, I was only 12 years old. I heard their screams as they were cut up with machetes by the community.

The army told us, "Look! Open your eyes! If you want to die in the same way, keep organizing, keep demanding your rights. Better that you each go your own way so that you won't all die. If you keep organizing you will die in the same way."

When it was over, the six were buried on the spot where they had been killed, in the cemetery. This happened in November 1982. Tthe community had just come out of hiding and returned to our village. Each year we celebrate the anniversary of these six martyrs, and others.

When I think of my father, and the martyrs in our community, I recall these words of Monsignor Romero that I heard from my father: "Martyrdom is a grace of God I don't deserve. But if God accepts the sacrifice of my life, may my blood be the seed of liberty and the sign that hope will one day soon become a reality."

In all, 55 people were killed in our community. These others were kidnapped by the army, or killed as they fled; some were burned alive. One man was crucified on a cross, and placed in a house that was then burned to the ground. He was burned alive. That happened in April 1982.

The Civil Defense Patrols (PACs)

What happened to us happened to many communities, perhaps in more horrible ways. Each community has its own story to tell. In most of the communities the army forced the people to kill their own people. It's tragic, because the soldiers are our own indigenous brothers. The policy and the plans are made by the high command of the army and the large landowners. But the ones who put these plans into practice are our own brothers.

So in November 1982, after the cruel death of the six catechists, we had to organize a civil defense patrol (PAC) in our village. I was part of the civil patrol. We had to carry out various projects, under order of the military commissioners and the civil patrol leaders in our municipality. We had to clear the roads, without receiving a single cent for our labor. We lost days doing this.

We were constantly threatened. The army threatened the military commissioners, who threatened the leaders of the civil patrols and they in turn threatened us. "Don't join any organization," they told us. "Whoever joins a popular organization will be kidnapped and killed."

The army, together with civil patrols from other villages, came to our community. The civil patrols were forced to help the army burn down houses and assassinate people. Little by little people in the community began to ask each other, "What are we going to do? Are we going to resist these threats? Are we going to resist this control?"

The Council of Ethnic Communities (CERJ)

In July 1899, the Runajel Junam Council of Ethnic Communities (CERJ) was formed to help indigenous people defend their constitutional right not to serve in the civil defense patrols. There have been many other examples of communities that have dissolved their civil patrols with the support of CERJ.

In our community it was difficult to do anything, even to meet to reflect on the Bible. Every day the military commissioners came to threaten us. Many widows were threatened, controlled, and even raped by the military commissioners and the leaders of the civil patrols. That's why CERJ was created in the first place.

With the support of CERJ we prepared our demand to the army. CERJ helped us write it, but the thoughts contained in the petition were our own. We took it to the Procurator for Human Rights, who then took it to the Ministry of Defense where General Héctor Alejandro Gramajo Morales signed it. The Procurator then sent a note to the army command post in Santa Cruz Quiché, informing them of the petition. That's when the army and the military commissioners came to our community again.

We Don't Want the Civil Patrol

I was there the day we decided to dissolve the civil patrol, and the army came to our community. The history of our community, the death of my father, all these things gave me strength to say, "Enough! We have to do something. If they kill me, just like they killed my father, fine. But we have to do something." We presented our demands as a community. We had elected a delegation of ten people, and each person spoke a few words. I was part of the delegation. I was very afraid, expecting to be killed.

We told the army, "We don't want the civil defense patrols (PACs) anymore." "Why," they asked us. "Because of our poverty. We can't afford to lose a day each week, working for the civil patrol. The cost of corn has risen." We had to serve 24 hours, one day a week in the civil patrol.

"But don't you see," the army replied, "that you're protecting your family and your community?" The army has convinced many people that the guerrillas are terrorists who will come to destroy the community. But it's really the army who does these things.

People in our community know better, because we witnessed how the army massacred us. It wasn't the guerrillas. But many people in other communities still believe it was the guerrillas who burned their houses and killed their people. They are ignorant of the truth, because the army has brainwashed them.

We were able to dissolve the civil patrol because our community is very organized. There are very few people who are not organized, and even these few do not oppose us or spy on us. The communities that have dissolved the civil patrols, with the help of CERJ, are organized communities, open communities. In our community the military commissioners no longer exist. We don't want them.

There used to be 650 people in our community; now there are 325. Many widows remarried. Many children are orphans, and do not receive the guidance that a parent could give. Many never have the opportunity to go to school; their mothers need them to work to help support the family. A family with one of the parents missing is like a house with only three pillars. No one has been left untouched by the violence.

Our Voice Has Not Been Silenced

Sometimes it amazes me that people want to hear the voice, to hear the testimony of indigenous people. I hope you will continue to hear the direct testimony of indigenous people who have lived in their own flesh the repression. Many times we indigenous people have never had this opportunity to give testimony, and we are quite capable of speaking for ourselves.

I hope this testimony can conscientize others about the reality of Guatemala. The government says, "There is peace in Guatemala, there is justice here." But if you ask an indigenous person, "What did you have to eat today?" they will tell you, "Salt, or chili." What does that signify? If you ask them, "How far in school did your children go?" they will reply, "No, we didn't have the opportunity to send our children to school. They had to stay home and work to support the family." We still live in extreme poverty.

I hope these testimonies will not be the only testimonies that are heard. I hope we can continue to share our experiences and coordinate our activities, so that others will join in solidarity with our people, our struggle, our hope, our organization. We are a people whose voice has not been silenced, a people whose voice grows stronger each day, but we need your solidarity.

Mexico At The Crossroads: The Martyrs Of Acteal

by Gonzalo Ituarte, O.P.

Since the January 1, 1994 rebellion of the Zapatistas in Chiapas, Mexico, the face of Chiapas has changed dramatically. Thousands of Mexican troops have occupied the state in a war of "low-intensity" against the mostly indigenous communities of the region. Negotiations between the Mexican government and the Zapatista rebels is at a standstill. The mediator of the conflict, Bishop Samuel Ruíz, has resigned his position, charging the Mexican government with a lack of sincerity. President Zedillo has refused to sign the San Andrés Accords which would give local autonomy to indigenous communities. And Zapatista communities continue to organize dozens of villages to begin establishing their own indigenous authority.

The village of Acteal, Chiapas, is just one example of the explosive situation that exists in Chiapas. People displaced from the war took refuge there because they desired peace. On December 22, 1997, paramilitary groups loyal to the local landowners and PRI Party cruelly massacred 45 men, women and children As they knelt to pray in the local chapel.

Father Gonzalo Ituarte, the Vicar General of the Diocese of San Cristobal de Las Casas and advisor to Bishop Samuel Ruíz, knew the victims of the December 22 massacre very well. He was their pastor, and mediator of the dialogue for peace between the political groups in the village. He offered the following interview to Brecha Magazine *in January 1998.*

We have begun to realize that what we witnessed was the martyrdom of a community whose faith was consecrated by prayer, three days of fasting, culminating in their unjust violent death. I knew the people in this community through my responsibility as a mediator between the two principal factions of the town: one side, which identified with the PRI, the political party

189

of the Mexican government; and the other side, which identified with the Zapatistas.

For some time now, the Zapatistas have been meeting in autonomous communities, trying to put into practice the San Andrés accords signed by both the Mexican government and the Zapatista Army of National Liberation (EZLN). These accords have not been fulfilled by the government nor put into law. The communities that support the Zapatistas are complying with the accords. They haven't signed them superficially; they want to put truth of their words into practice, and they are trying to establish an autonomous government according to their indigenous customs.

How did the conflict in Acteal get started?

The leaders of Acteal have said that they are not going to permit anyone to live here who does not belong to the PRI Party. Those who identify with the Zapatistas will be expelled unless they join the PRI; and those who wish to return to the town under these conditions will have to pay a fine of $100. In Acteal there is a group of nonviolent people called *"las abejas"*—this is the group that was killed in the chapel—who have refused to join either side.

What is taking place in Chiapas is a form of political cleansing, similar to the ethnic cleansing in Bosnia. There is a clear rupture within Mexico, between Mexican society and the indigenous people, that has erupted into brutal violence. But it is evident to us that this kind of violence goes beyond that which has traditionally existed within these community. It clearly points to psychological manipulation and even paramilitary training by those who foment this kind of violence.

We know, for example, that a conflict has been building since May 1997 in this Tzotzil region of northern Chiapas between several towns. The violence began with the appearance of a paramilitary group in Los Chorros, the most populated part of the region. Since then, shots have been heard almost every night. Denunciations have been made about an Army lieutenant who came here from Zacatecas, in northern Mexico, to recruit young people as paramilitaries, with the purpose of training them in the use of weapons. These meetings usually ended in dances with prostitutes.

The diabolical dimension of this war is that it has resulted in brothers and sisters killing each other. If you compare the names of the victims with the names of their assassins, you find the same clans, the same last names; they are neighbors and even relatives in some cases. The war has become a war against the people of the most perverse sort, abusing economic resources that were destined for productive development but now are used for the purpose of death.

Is anybody going to investigate what happened at Acteal?

The attitude of the government, at least at the level of words, is one of condemnation of the massacre. But their attitude also reflects the principal concern of the authorities is to protect the image of the state and federal governments, and avoid pointing the finger at high officials in power. This is their attitude, instead of passionately defending the life of the poorest Mexicans, who are the indigenous peoples.

During the most recent past, we have seen a government in Chiapas that is firmly entrenched against the Indians. So today, they are concerned first with defending political personalities and party and government officials, because this is the priority of those who are in power, not the life of the people. In this drama there are moral, political and intellectual players who should be judged for conspiring against the peace process in Chiapas.

The massacre at Acteal should not be limited to a judicial or police investigation. Acteal presents the people of Mexico with a moral challenge, namely, to reflect on the significance of the massacre in light of events in Latin America during the 1970s and the recent drama in Central America in the 1980s. Mexico needs a moral reflection; we cannot afford to fall into the whirlpool of indifference in the face of the death of innocent people, of women, children, and elderly who were praying in church, a place of sanctuary for refugees, and where they were robbed of their lives.

Who was actually responsible for the massacre?

Among the aggressors there were those who have been methodically opposed to the peace process and negotiations in the municipal region of Chenalho. We have denounced this. Those who boycotted the negotiations in Chenalho were members of the PRI party, as well as people from the Frente Cardenista, a corrupt and Mafia-like group. One week before the massacre, the Frente Cardenista publicly threatened to go to Acteal.

There was another interesting occurrence. On October 2, the municipal president of Chenalho, Jacinto Arias, asked President Ernesto Zedillo, when he was here in San Cristobal, if he would permit the local PRI officials to carry weapons to defend themselves from the Zapatistas. Since then the public security police have provided them with arms.

The greatest tragedy is that the Mexican government has lost sight of the very function for which it was founded, to serve the common good. When that happens, the government ends up destroying itself by destroying everybody who opposes it. The inability of the government to receive and accept criticism ends up by converting it into a monster.

What happens now?

We are at a crossroads. The massacre at Acteal is a point that marks a change of direction in the social, political and military phenomena of Chiapas. Without a doubt. We don't know where this will lead. The paramilitary groups in Chenalho, like other death squads that operate with impunity in the region, are generated, supported, and encouraged by government officials. I think, by this savage behavior, the Mexican government has been stripped naked before its free trade allies and completely lost control.

All this has generated a psychosis, an insanity within the paramilitary groups; once they were unleashed they were unable to be controlled. But even when we did warn the authorities about what was happening—I personally informed the local government minister that a violent attack had begun in Acteal—they still did not intervene to stop the massacre. For several hours they let the paramilitaries do as they please.

Since the massacre, there has been a substantial increase of military presence in the region. The Army has solicited lands in order to build a military base in the town of Polho, a Zapatista rebel community. This leads us to believe that the massacre at Acteal was part of a counterinsurgency strategy typical of low-intensity conflicts.

How did the December 22 massacre at Acteal affect you personally?

It affected me very profoundly. Acteal was the only community in Chenalho with which I was personally involved in giving aid to the refugees. My usual place of work had been with other neighboring towns and the jungle of Ocosingo. In Chenalho, however, I went to the little chapel in Acteal. That's where I met the people who were martyred. I knew them as refugees who had fled the violence, people committed to nonviolence.

Holy Week In
El Salvador:
The Cross
Of A Crucified People

by Jon Sobrino, S.J.

In El Salvador, as in much of Central America, Good Friday is more popular than Easter Sunday. Why is this so? Perhaps because the poor have so strongly identified the suffering of Jesus on the cross with their own cruel and unjust suffering. The Way of the Cross is not simply a religious devotion but a lived reality in which the poor—united by their faith and suffering to Jesus— are the principal protagonists. It is this reality that inspired Ignacio Ellacuria, one of the six Jesuit martyrs in El Salvador, to speak of the poor as "a crucified people." The mystery of our faith is that from this cross come light and salvation for the world. Life, not death, has the last word.

Jon Sobrino is a Jesuit theologian and Director of the Oscar Romero Pastoral Center in San Salvador. He was a friend of the six Jesuit martyrs who are buried just a short distance from his office. The following article appeared in the 1991 edition of Letter to the Churches, *published by the Central American University (UCA) in San Salvador and translated by CRISPAZ.*

I have been asked to write a few pages on "how to preach the cross to the crucified" and I am going to do so from my experience in El Salvador, home of a truly crucified people. But first I would like to say that this is the kind of question that has the capacity to express the fundamental elements of our faith and of our historical situation. Because of its importance and the difficulty in answering it, it is a question very similar to that of the first Christians: "How is it possible that one who was crucified could bring salvation?" It is similar to the question that Gustavo Gutierrez considers central to theology today: "How can we say to the poor that God loves them?" And it is a question in which are expressed such fundamental Christian thoughts as "sin is powerful" and the ultimate hope that "grace may be stronger than sin."

We believe that all of these things are part of the question. And the answer, therefore, is not just a pastoral or homiletic matter, nor can the answer be routine. It is rather the ever-unfinished task and the knowing that there is definitively never a convincing response using only words and concepts. Yet, as faith tells us that we must preach the cross, and reality shows us that there are crucified ones, there must be a response to the question. We believe that today it is possible to preach the cross if we do it with truth, with the conviction of the Good News and with credibility.

Preaching the Cross with Truth

Jesus did not die a natural death nor much less an easy death. He was executed as a political malefactor. He was executed because he disturbed all of the powers that made society an oppressor of the poor and weak. The well-known but important conclusion in this: in history there is a terrible evil that has power—the Malignant One in transcendentalized language; high priests, the rich, scribes, Herodians, Pharisees, and Pilate in historicized language. Those powers are in the service of the configuration of society for personal gain and against the weak. So, if Jesus announced and initiated the Kingdom of God, those powers proclaim and construct the anti-Kingdom. In the times of Jesus, this was a theocracy around the temple and the imperial Pax Romana—both oppressors of the majority.

And to this well-known truth must be added the fact that Jesus also died as a blasphemer and he was put to death in the name of a god: "the living God," in whose name, ironically, the high priest denounces him, "the Caesar" invoked by the Jews before Pilate. Jesus dies at the hands of idols, real and existing divinities that demand victims in order to subsist.

This is the simple and terrifying truth about the death of Jesus. There is a force in history that frontally opposes the Kingdom of God, justice, truth and fraternity. And that opposition kills all of the mediators of the Kingdom and kills even the mediator Jesus, the one sent by God to announce the Kingdom. The first and great truth of the cross of Jesus is then, that sin exists, that sin really kills and that even the Son of God succumbs to that power of sin.

The cross of Jesus is not the only cross in history. Many before and many after him die crucified. In El Salvador Monsignor Romero and Ignacio Ellacuria have died violently. And above all, many peasants and indigenous people have died in an anonymous way because of unjust poverty. They are the poor majority of the Third World whom Ignacio Ellacuria called "the crucified peoples" and he compared them to be the suffering servant of Yahweh who dies disfigured and without a human face, defenseless and without a word, without even a worthy tomb.

To speak of the cross today signifies speaking the truth about our peoples and saying it with greater clarity than the terms of other languages: "the Third World," the "South" or the euphemisms that are used to twist the truth: "developing countries," or "incipient democracies." The preaching of the cross must first unmask these lies.

In effect, "crucified peoples" signifies people that die. This death is above all the slow death of poverty, and in Latin America we are experiencing greater poverty. In 1970 there were 71 million poor and in 1990 there were 183 million, according to the data of the UN Economic Commission on Latin America (ECLA). "Crucified peoples" signifies people who are actively and violently killed. They do not fall from heaven, and if you followed the inertia of the metaphor you would rather have to say that they rose up from hell. And they are killed violently when, in order to live, they organize themselves and even fight justly. In El Salvador there are 75,000 dead and in Guatemala 200,000.

And in these people there is something central that makes them appear like Christ crucified, to the extent that in looking at them, we know Christ better. "You are the image of the divine incarnated", said Monsignor Romero to some terrorized peasants who had survived a massacre.

This is then, the truth of the cross in our world, a terrible truth that some wish to hide and cover—as if things were not so bad—and which some also wish to twist—as if the responsibility were with the poor themselves for having chosen the wrong path for improving their lot. To preach the cross with truth is, above all, to pronounce judgement on the sinful world.

Preaching the Cross with Good News

If what has been said here is not easy to say because of the conflicts it causes, it is much more difficult to preach the cross as the Good News because of the scandal it produces. And, nevertheless, this is essential for the Christian preaching of the cross.

The first Christians were disconcerted by the cross of Jesus, although they had the immense courage to maintain it in all of its radicalness. Thus, the tradition of Mark presents a failed Jesus on the cross, abandoned by his followers and abandoned by God. The first Christians did not know how to explain the why of the cross, although they attempted it by saying that his was the death of a prophet foretold in the Scriptures. But they ended up saying the only thing they could say: The cross is the plan of God and only God understands the why of the cross.

And here resounds the great question even today: How can the cross of Jesus be the plan of a good God, of a God so close to Jesus that he is called Father? In today's words, how can the cross be the plan of a God of life, of a God of the poor, of a God of liberation?

The answer of the New Testament is that the cross of Jesus brings much good; it is salvation from sin and to explain it theologians have developed diverse theories: the cross is sacrifice, vicarious expiation, blood of the new covenant. But there is not much here that convinces, until we hear the simple and profound and fundamental words of Paul and John: The cross is the manifestation of love.

They said that on the cross was demonstrated the ultimate love of Jesus who "went doing good and liberating all the oppressed," that the mercy and the solidarity of Jesus are manifested—it takes him where it may—in defense of the poor and the victims. And they said that in the cross is manifested the love of God: "For God so loved the world, he gave his only begotten Son."

These are scandalous words, cruel on the one hand, and blessed on the other. God had no other way to say that he is in our favor than by letting his Son be in our favor to the very end. The "God with us" in the birth of Jesus, the "God for us" in the announcement of the Kingdom, on the cross is made a "God at our mercy." And in this way he shows us love.

Human beings, the poor and the victims above all, could ask themselves why they would want a love that is impotent on the cross. But they at least understand very well the credibility of that love: Jesus was like us and for us to the very end and God himself left him on the cross to demonstrate that in his incarnation he is absolutely real.

That the cross produces fruit and is good news for the poor of this world cannot be decided in advance, nor is it enough to repeat traditional doctrines. But it is accumulated experience that a believable love does bear fruit. And so, with the assassination of Monsignor Romero the poor certainly lost a great defender but not all was lost: even today they remember him with thankfulness and affection without equal. They are imbued with hope and vitality for the work and the struggle. And all of this because in the death of Monsignor Romero, accepted by him in advance when he had rejected the security offered to him, they saw a great love. And this is because a great love always yields fruit.

The cross of Jesus must be preached as good news according to the Christian faith but we must see if in the crosses of today's poor there is some good news. The question itself is terrifying and we can only attempt to give a response with fear and trembling. Above all, it must be said that the crosses of today demonstrate the "failure" to which we have subjected God, since if God tolerated and suffered the cross of his Son, it was so that the cross would not be repeated in history. Nevertheless, the crosses of history exist and it must be asked if and what good they bring. For this, let us return to the Suffering Servant whom the Scriptures call "light" and "salvation." And not only that but also that he is the "elected one" of God for bringing that light and that salvation.

There is here, again, a scandalous truth, but there is also an irony because the crucified people are present as the Good News, above all for others, for those of us who are not poor and victims like them. What of this is there in the crucified peoples of the present?

Above all, the crucified people are "light" for all the nations. They uncover the truth of this world and tear off the mask of lies to which they are subjected. In them, as in an inverted mirror, the nations see their true realty. And with that light, the crucified people also propose the true utopia for the world today, distant from the consumerist and dehumanizing progress—with which the powers of this world want to imbue us—and centered in shared austerity.

And they are also "salvation." The crucified peoples move all to conversion, and if they do not attain this, nothing can. They also offer, through being poor and with greater innateness than others, a gospel "the evangelizing potential" of which Puebla speaks: solidarity, service, simpleness and readiness to embrace the gift of God. They offer hope, foolish or absurd or because it is the only thing that remains to them one could say; but there is their hope and a type of hope that moves history in the correct and humanizing direction. They offer forgiveness to those who come close to help them, and thus—paradoxically and simultaneously—their oppressors come to know themselves as sinners and forgiven. They know themselves in their reality but with an open future. They generate solidarity, a way of living and a mutual understanding between human beings, open to each other for giving and receiving the best from each other.

Finally they offer a faith, a more truthful and Christian way of being a Church and a holiness, more relevant for the present world and better able to recuperate Jesus of Nazareth. This is what the crucified of history offer us as good news. And this is why Ignacio Ellacuria insisted on speaking of the suffering servant in whom must be elaborated a "historical soteriology" (the theological doctrine of salvation). That there is salvation in the crucified is a scandalous affirmation of faith, but it is also true.

Preaching the Cross with Credibility

How to preach the cross to the crucified and how to make that cross good news for them in the question being dealt with in this article. The response cannot be just theory but must be essentially praxis, and in this praxis two things seem essential to us:

"My servant will prosper," says Isaiah. The cross of Jesus can only be preached as good news—without this becoming mockery—if at the same time we commit ourselves to lowering the poor from their crosses. Ignacio Ellacuria paraphrased three fundamental questions about Christ crucified from Saint Ignatius. Let us place ourselves before the crucified peoples and ask ourselves: "What have we done to put them on the cross?" "What are we doing as we stand before their crosses?" "What are we going to do to lower them from their cross?"

Without this decided readiness to lower them from the cross we cannot speak to them today about the cross of Christ nor of their own cross. It would be a mockery, historically, to preach the Good News to them without working to change their terrible reality. It would be a radical lack of faith in the resurrection since, although it sounds strange and callous, it is up to us, of course in a historic way, to do with the crucified what God did with the just and innocent crucified Jesus: to return him to life. And it would be useless pastorally, since the crucified are fed up with deceitful promises and they no longer listen only to words.

And we must be clear about what we are doing when we speak of readiness to lower them from their crosses. We are not doing anything but returning the Good News to the crucified, the light and salvation that they are for us. To do this we must preach the cross above all with effective thankfulness toward those who carry our sins and who thus illuminate and save us.

With this readiness, the cross of Jesus can be preached to the crucified with credibility. Without credibility the word of the cross would not be only a routine word but also cruel. This credibility is engendered in the praxis of lowering them from their crosses, and in the readiness to carry their crosses ourselves since it is essential to faith that sin must be carried to eradicate it. The readiness to accept the conflicts, the threats, the persecution and death itself is what carrying the crucifying sins of the world signifies historically. It is what gives credibility to the preaching of the cross.

Monsignor Romero said it clearly: "I do not want security as long as it is not given to my people." He did not want security and he lost his life, but in so doing he achieved credibility. He was able to accomplish the miracle of preaching the cross of Jesus to his people and the miracle of their acceptance of his message.

To preach the cross is definitely an act of love, and no dogma, theology, or pastoral approach can replace that love. It is a love for the crucified, a love that speaks the truth, that cries out against the crosses, that denounces the crucifiers and unmasks the causes of the cross. It is a love that encourages the crucified to be conscious and organize themselves and struggle themselves. It is a love that participates in their crosses and in the defenselessness before them. It is a love that ends up crucified.

It is the love of Jesus to the end and it is the total love of Jesus. Monsignor Romero love the crucified of his people and he loved them without any other intention. (For us it is often the case that in the defense of the crucified, we also keep in mind the defense of our own party, of our own Church). A love like his is credible. With such a love, the cross can be preached. And with a love like that we can also preach the hope that the resurrection is possible, which is what God—and they—want for the crucified.

There are no recipes for preaching the cross to the crucified but yes, there are conditions: the credibility of love. What happens afterwards, that the preaching of the cross becomes real and also scandalously good news for the crucified is a thing to be verified. In Latin America this often happens.

The crucified Jesus, so close and in solidarity with the crucified, continues to produce more hope than resignation, more liberating action than inaction. And in our opinion this happens when the crucified of today see Christ in other human beings who have loved the poor, have worked with them, have defended them and have died like them.

Therefore, to respond to the question with which we began: From El Salvador I have nothing better to say than these words: Today the cross can be preached but we must preach it as did Tilo and Polin, Silvia and Ticha, Ignacio Ellacuria and Monsignor Romero.

The Legacy Of Oscar Romero: Who Will Tend The Roses Now?

by Bishop Pedro Casaldáliga

One of the impressive legacies left to us by more decades of war in Central America, Mexico and the Caribbean is the witness of the martyrs. Each of them has endured in their life great suffering, and each has demonstrated great love: that is what makes them martyrs, in the popular sense. In the words of Jon Sobrino, "Where great suffering and great love converge, we are standing on holy ground." Perhaps no other martyr is so well-loved and so much revered as Archbishop Oscar Romero, the martyred pastor of El Salvador. In his life he demonstrated great love and great courage as he made of his life and ministry a preferential option for the poor. He became in his death what he was in his life, a source of light and salvation to the world.

In the following reflection, Brazilian Bishop Pedro Casaldáliga offers a tribute to Archbishop Romero on the occasion of the fifteenth anniversary of his martyrdom. His talk was given in March 1995 during the annual Romero commemoration at the Central American University (UCA) in San Salvador.

On this fifteenth anniversary, I think it is very important that we gather up the legacy of Oscar Romero. I insist on this because Monsignor Romero was a man and a saint of his time; he knew how to open himself faithfully to the signs of his time and place and respond to them—even unto martyrdom. Sometimes we can isolate our saints, but we shouldn't—especially not the political ones. Political in the most beautiful sense of the word. Do you know what Pope Paul VI used to say? That politics is the highest expression of Christian love.

Romero became a saint mainly because he responded to the circumstances of his time. Human circumstances, made of flesh and weeping and struggle, conflict and hope. He responded to his people. These days a typical Romero phrase is going around: "The people are my prophet." I don't know why I am telling you that because you all know it was the people who sanctified him.

I think that sainthood would partly be that: responding to the place and time according to the spirit of God. And we want to gather up his heritage and his time. In time, right? Because you all know that it's when they aren't a disturbance anymore that they are canonized. We want to canonize him while he's still a disturbance, no? We want to extend and prolong the legacy of Romero and his lifetime.

A Difficult Lent for Central America

We are in Lent, a time of desert and a time of temptation. We are living through a difficult Lent with political and social consequences this days. It's because of the fall of the utopias, no? The dark night of liberation. We have been overwhelmed by neoliberalism: the end of history. The utopias are gone. That's very real and dramatic, no? Our people do not live fully, they barely survive. But you all know this from your own experience. During this Lent that is more difficult than ever, I think we face a triple temptation, the three temptations of Jesus: the temptation to renounce memory, the temptation to renounce the cross, the temptation to renounce utopia.

To renounce memory would be to renounce faith, because our faith is a historic faith. We believe in a God who made history, don't we? To renounce the cross would be to renounce love because the greatest proof of love is to climb up and embrace the cross. And to renounce utopia is a clear one; it would be to renounce hope. So there is a triple temptation that is cutting at the roots of our theology, which is our Christian life. I'm going to try to be explicit here.

First, let me say something about memory. I don't know to what extent we can speak about peace when there is no justice. I am reminded of the prophets, when they cried out against the talk of "Peace, peace," when there was no peace! Jesus also emphasized that his peace is not of this world. Under the subterfuge of peace, of amnesty, we are asked to forget the torture, the massacres, the colonization, even their hunger and misery. Quite often official amnesty is official amnesia. We know how all the empires and the torturers and the usual dominators have bent over backwards to erase people's memory.

Second, let us look at the temptation to renounce the cross. Quality of life is being proclaimed as the ideal for human society. This is the sociopolitical, economic, cultural theological proposal of the First World, no? Yet, all over the world we lack even the minimum conditions of life, no?

Moreover, God wants a maximum of well being for all. The kingdom of God is the maximum of well-being.

And finally, utopia. The rich want to convince us that we have come to the end of history: There are no more utopias. But for the vast majority of human beings, history is not even possible for them. Today, the poor are not only those who have been impoverished, but those who have been excluded.

Eduardo Galeano has a beautiful parable about the goal of utopia. In one of his books, Angel stands in front of the horizon. As he walks towards the horizon, the horizon keeps receding. Finally, he stops. Tired, he asks, "What is this horizon good for?" And the voice, which might be God's voice, answers, "It keeps you walking!" The horizon is our utopia, no? It keeps us walking. If there were no utopia, there would be no future for humanity. We are people of the future. God, our God, is our future.

The Glory of God is the Poor Fully Alive

You know that Saint Romero got along well with Saint Irenaeus when it came to defining the glory of God, right? For Saint Irenaeus, the glory of God was "human beings fully alive." For Romero, it was "the poor fully alive." Our Saint Romero was a little more complete and radical, no?

Well, confronted with these temptations, we—like Jesus our brother who overcame temptation—must offer a clear answer. I marvel when I imagine that here in our America, specifically our Central America, hundreds of thousands have given their lives. We are what we remember: We are genes, we are legacy, we are culture, we are history. The memory of a people is its history.

As Christians, we are children of the Great Memory. The Church itself should be, above all, the historicized, enculturated, and, yes, politicized memorial to Jesus. Jesus left us two commands that make us Church: "Love one another as I have loved you," and "Do this in memory of me."

The Subversive Memory of Jesus

It seems much more real than symbolic to me that Saint Romero died celebrating the Eucharist. He was celebrating the subversive memory of Jesus. And he himself remains with us as a subversive memory.

Jesus asks that we do this in his memory: Break his body, pour out his blood, do this in memory of him. Live this Passover in memory of him. You know very well that Jesus' Passover is our Passover. What we do as Christians is celebrate Eucharist without getting our hands dirty. I think that more than once we have washed our hands like Pilate, no?

Nor is it easy to consecrate the Host. It's simple to lift the chalice of wine. But to gather the flesh and blood of the people—their cries, their suffering, their impotence, their shouts, their hunger, their disconnectedness, their disorganization, even their unfaithfulness: Isn't that the crushed body and blood of Christ in the people? That's much more difficult to do.

The Challenge of Romero's Legacy Today

Gathering together the legacy of Monsignor Romero means making Romero's commitments our own; beginning with his perspective and his pastoral approach and bearing witness to it today in a dynamic way. The three temptations—to renounce memory, to renounce the cross, and to renounce utopia—are moments of crisis, of growth, but they could also be seen as a moments of *kairos,* and of God's grace.

That's why our memory must also invite repentance. Perhaps we have oppressed people by trying to impose liberation. We must try to build community at the same time that we work with the people. Perhaps we have been a elitist in our relationships. We should participate in the life of the people and try to make every effort to respond to the needs, even the most basic needs, of the people.

Be Leaven Among the Leaven: What else must we do? Sometimes we make plans based on ideas and on programs, instead of being based on real life. Of course, we should be leaven in the dough, but we should also be leaven among the leaven: in the Church, in the university, in the popular movement, in the labor unions, in the FMLN. There's a lot of leaven that has gone bad. What good is leaven that is sealed up and stored away? Jesus tells us that if it becomes insipid and the leaven doesn't rise, we must multiply the leaven. We must multiply our communities.

Bring Life and Liberation Together: We should announce the essential message of our faith through the witness of our lives. I think especially now in this time of disillusionment and disunity we should learn to simplify our Christianity to the most essential elements. That's where our theologians have done us a favor recently, reminding us insistently about the value of life, the defense of life, the God of life. Here on our continent, we need to bring life and liberation together.

Awaken Hope Among the People: We need to awaken hope! Listen, if there is something to admire about Monsignor Romero, it's that he inspired hope, right? I believe that he spent his three years as archbishop in the Garden of Gethsemene. Yet he never lost hope. When Romero was archbishop, solidarity was awakening in and with Central America. We need to continue to nurture the values of our people, their capacity for hospitality, their capacity for celebration, the value they place on the land, on God, on prayer. Maybe we do too much head work and not enough knee work.

Be Critical and Self-Critical: We shouldn't canonize the people, right? We should help people become familiar with their mistakes, their desire for an immediate solution, their fanaticism about leaders and authorities. Last year, ARENA won the election in El Salvador. This year there's a possibility that Ríos Montt could win the elections in Guatemala. People want security at any price.

To Nurture the Ideals of Our People

The legacy of Monsignor Romero and his time—culturally, socially, politically, and economically—is fundamentally a Latin American legacy. The legacy is ours, because this is our place, and this is our hour.

But for us to be able to live Romero's legacy, we need to denounce the idolatry of neoliberalism. The Church should repent now, before it's too late, because at opportune moments we have failed to explicitly condemn neoliberalism as sinful and idolatrous. Otherwise, we will have to do so in the future. Neoliberalism is killing us all.

Let's not be afraid to raise the banners of utopia, for the love of God. If we don't, who will? When all the utopias have all fallen, God forbid, at least there will be one left standing: the kingdom of God, which is the utopia of Jesus.

Now You Must Tend the Roses

Finally, we need to be united, wherever we may be. There are greater things—like that legacy we have in common—that unite us rather than those that divide us. When I found out about the death of Obdulio, the husband of Julia Elba and the father of Celina who were murdered with the six Jesuits in 1989, I recalled how he used to take care of the roses in the garden where the Jesuits are buried, and I wondered, "Who will take care of the roses now?"

It's up to all of you to take care of those roses. That is the challenge for all of us, especially for all of you young people. It is the challenge of the roses and the thorns. It is a challenge for El Salvador, to bear witness and remain faithful to the memory of your prophet, Oscar Romero; it's a challenge, also, to remain faithful to your vocation as a prophetic people. That's what you are, right? Light, salt, leaven, and hope for all of us.

VIII

Solidarity
For The
New
Millennium

Speaking Truth
To Power:
The School Of
The Americas

Court Testimonies from the Defendants

The School of the Americas (SOA) at Fort Benning, Georgia is a US Army combat training school, funded by US taxpayers, exclusively for training Latin American military personnel. Founded in 1946 in Panama, it was moved to Fort Benning in 1984. The SOA has trained some of the worst human rights violators in Latin America, including those who were responsible for the massacre of hundreds of men, women and children in El Mozote, El Salvador, the four US church women in El Salvador, and the six Jesuits and two women, also in El Salvador. The following testimonies were taken from the trials and sentencing of the 25 defendants who crossed the line onto the base in November 1997, calling for the school to be closed down as a national disgrace. They were subsequently sentenced to six months in prison each.

Testimony of Father Roy Bourgeois

Roy Bourgeois, 59, is a Maryknoll priest from Lutcher, Louisiana, who worked as a missioner in Bolivia. Before his ordination in 1972, he was a US Naval officer who received the Purple Heart during the Vietnam War. Currently, he heads SOA Watch, a grassroots movement headquartered in Columbus, GA, which monitors human rights abuses of graduates of the US Army School of the Americas at Fort Benning.

Your Honor, we are not bank robbers. It hurt to hear the prosecuting attorney comparing us to bank robbers. We are a people of faith. We are a people of conscience. We are a people of goodwill. Most of us here before you have spent time among our sisters and brothers in Latin America. I speak for myself. This is the fourth time I am before you in this court. You have sent me to prison now for over three years. What is it that makes me keep coming back? I think it's the same experience that we share in common today. It's our experience in Latin America.

It really hurt me and it angered me to hear the prosecuting attorneys say that the School of the Americas is not the issue. It is the issue that brought us here. Soldiers from Latin America, trained down the road, just four miles from here, are responsible for the death, the rape, the torture of countless people in Latin America. And it hurt me to hear that that's not the issue.

But really, at the very core of this issue, the starting point is not the School of the Americas. The starting point is the reality of Latin America. And that reality is about poverty. It is about people struggling for food for the table. This is not a complicated issue, Your Honor. It's a very, very simple one. It's not about crossing the line; it's about that reality of poverty. Parents who are trying to get schools for their children, medicines, adequate housing. People who see their children die before their time, before 3 or 4 years old. That's the starting point of this issue. And that's why we are here. We have heard those stories. We have documented those atrocities of graduates of the School of the Americas. And we are women and men of faith, of conscience who are aware of this reality. And it's that reality that brought us here.

Prison is a hard and lonely place. I've been there. Others have been there. And I have to say this, Your Honor, if you believe that these harsh sentences and outrageous fines that we cannot pay will kill this movement of people from around the country which has come to Columbus, Georgia, it won't work!

You will only energize us and more people to come here. We will not be silent. We will not shut up. We will not go away. We go to prison empowered by the martyrs, the victims of the graduates of the School of the Americas, those thugs that we bring here to train. What I've heard here today against us reminds me of Isaiah: "Let's take an evil and call it good; let's take a lie and call it the truth." The words of Isaiah came alive in this courtroom over the last couple of days. Taking an evil and turning it into a good. A lie into the truth.

It won't work. People of faith, people in this country are more educated. They know better. And I can only say that we go to prison empowered by people like Jean Donovan, Dorothy Kazel, my friends, Ita Ford and Maura Clarke, missionary women from the United States who have been raped and killed by graduates of the School of the Americas.

Your Honor, the truth cannot be silenced. You're going to send us around this country to federal prisons where it's hard, where it's lonely. We'll be cut off from our loved ones and our friends, and it's going to hurt. But we will not be quiet. We will speak from our prisons.

And I think it is so wrong, as our attorney said, so very very wrong. Something is wrong here today when we, people of faith, advocates of non-violence who participate in a solemn silent funeral procession, carrying coffins to remember those killed, to remember the 15-year-old girl, her mother and those Jesuits, killed by graduates of the school, when we carry those white crosses bearing the names of the victims, we go to prison. And when those who did the killing are given amnesty and will not see one day behind bars, there is a problem, a travesty of justice.

And lastly, I just want to say when we serve out our sentences, when we get through these difficult days and months ahead, we're coming back. We're not going away. We will not be silent. We are going to come back in greater numbers until that school of death, that school of horror here in Columbus, Georgia, the school that brings shame upon this community, upon our armed forces and upon us, is closed! We are going to be back!

Testimony of Carol Richardson

Carol Richardson, 53, is a United Methodist minister and director of the SOA Watch office in Washington, D.C. A justice and peace activist for 20 years, she has visited the refugee camps in Chiapas, Mexico, and the refugee resettlement communities in Guatemala. As a minister, Richardson served parishes in Ohio and Maryland. She is the mother of two children.

Your Honor, on November 16, over 2,000 people gathered at Fort Benning's main gate, and over 600 of us walked onto Fort Benning in a solemn funeral procession. Despite what the prosecutor and the Fort Benning lawyer have implied, I want to be clear that this was a silent, respectful event.

We came that day to honor all those in Latin America who have suffered the brutal consequences of the School of the America's training. And we came especially to commemorate two women and six Jesuit priests who were assassinated in El Salvador in 1989. Nineteen of the 26 Salvadoran officers responsible for this atrocity were trained at US taxpayer expense at the School of the Americas located at Fort Benning. This is a fact verified by the United Nations Truth Commission.

The murder of the six Jesuits and two women is one horrifying example of the work of SOA graduates. Consistently, those trained at the SOA have left a trail of blood and suffering in every Latin American country where they have returned.

We Make the Road By Walking

On November 16, we marched into Fort Benning because we believe we have a moral responsibility to try to close this death machine called the School of the Americas, and we marched onto Fort Benning because we believe we have a First Amendment right to be there to speak our criticisms. Supporters of the SOA regularly are invited on base to speak in favor of the school. They are not arrested, and they certainly are not sent to prison. Why are we?

On November 16, my friends and I carried small white crosses as we walked in the funeral procession. Each cross bore the name of an SOA victim. I carried a cross with the name of someone I knew—Juan Lopez. That's not entirely true. I never knew Juan, but I did meet his mother in 1988 in Quilali, a little village in northern Nicaragua. I was there with a group of 20 other churchpeople. We wanted to find out firsthand what the US-funded *Contra* War was all about and especially what effect it was having on ordinary people, particularly the poor.

As I was walking through town, a woman spotted my camera and asked me if I would come to her house and take a picture of her and her son. I waited outside while she went in, I thought, to get her son. But when she came out, no one followed. Instead, she brought a photo of Juan.

You see, Your Honor, her son Juan was 15—about the same age as my son—when he was kidnapped, tortured and murdered by the *Contras*. His mother found his body thrown like garbage in front of their house. She did not have a picture of the two of them together, so she held up his picture beside her face and asked me to take a photo of her and the picture of her son.

The SOA trained over 4,000 Nicaraguan soldiers that became Somoza's death squads. These soldiers were the backbone and leaders of the US-backed *Contras* who murdered, tortured and raped thousands of Nicaraguans. Juan Lopez was one, and I carried a cross on November 16 to honor him and all the others and their families who have suffered because of this School of Assassins.

So you see, Your Honor, I could not *not* walk in the funeral procession on November 16. And I believe that if you had seen what I have seen and heard the stories that I have heard and known those whom I have known, like Juan's mother—if you had seen and heard and known as I have, then I believe, Your Honor, that you would have walked with us.

Testimony of Sister Rita Steinhagen

Rita Steinhagen, 70, a Sister of St. Joseph of Carondelet, serves at the Center for Victims of Torture in Minneapolis, Minnesota. Since 1969, she has worked with refugees, homeless persons, runaways and battered women. In 1987, she spent eight months in Nicaragua as a Witness for Peace.

I'm a Sister of Saint Joseph of Carondelet. I've been a Sister for 47 years, and I belong to a wonderful organization. Ten members of my religious community have come here to support me today. I would like to begin with a statement by Archbishop Desmond Tutu, who said, "If you are neutral in situations of injustice, you have chosen the side of the oppressor. If an elephant has his foot on the tail of a mouse and you say that you are neutral, the mouse will not appreciate it."

I am here today because I am not neutral. I'm also here today because I know of great injustices that have been inflicted on those small countries of Latin America. I have lived in Guatemala and Nicaragua, and I have seen the sufferings of these people. I'm also here today especially for the four churchwomen who were brutally murdered and raped in El Salvador in 1980, citizens of the United States of America. Five of the Salvadoran officers cited in that case were trained right here at the School of the Americas at Fort Benning, Georgia. None of them has spent one day in prison.

The graduates of the School of the Americas are notorious for their cruelty, often raping and torturing before they murder. One article stated there has been a trail of blood and suffering in every Latin America country where School of the Americas graduates have returned. An editorial in *The New York Times* in September 1996 stated: "An institution so clearly out of tune with American values should be shut down without delay."

For the past six years, I have worked with clients from the Center for Victims of Torture, located in Minneapolis. There are over 400,000 victims of torture living in the United States. Approximately 12,000 of those live in Minnesota. These clients come from all over the world. Some of them come from countries whose personnel have been trained right here at the School of the Americas. I have seen marks of torture on their bodies and I have heard their stories.

I am appalled and I am ashamed to know that in some sense, I am the cause of their suffering and their pain because it is my country that is training their soldiers and it's my tax dollars and your tax dollars that pay for the training of these soldiers.

How can I remain neutral? How can anyone remain neutral when they know that such a place as the School of the Americas is causing such pain and suffering to so many people in so many countries? It is beyond the time that *that* school be shut down.

Your Honor, I have never been in prison. Today, on my 70th birthday, I suspect I will get sentenced. I guess that's a new stage of my life. But I tell you: I am more fearful of what is going on in this country than I am of going to prison. It is an absolute outrage when people such as we and people supporting us can sit here and listen to what has gone on in this courtroom. I am scared of what is going on in this country. I don't know what else I can do about it, but believe me, as long as I live, I will do my best.

Testimony of Judith Williams

Judith Williams, 58, is executive director of the Waukesha Catholic Worker in Waukesha, Wisconsin. Former director of music therapy at St. Mary's Hill Hospital in Milwaukee, and at St. Teresa's College in Winona, Minnesota, she is the mother of three grown children and grandmother of six.

My name is Judith Williams, and I'm the executive director of the Waukesha Catholic Worker. We bring people from Central America for surgery in our affluent area. We feel a committedness and connectedness to Central America.

With some of the people in this courtroom, the Sages and Linda and Bob, I was in El Salvador recently, within the last two months. And there I met with Rufina Amaya. We spent the day with Rufina. And she has—or had—four children, who were killed by graduates of the School of the Americas: 9-year-old Cristina, 5-year-old Maria Delores, 3-year-old Martita, and 8-month-old Maria Isabel.

Now, I'm a grandma, and I have three children and six grandchildren. And my youngest daughter is breast-feeding my little grandson. His name is Jacob. And on December 11, 1981, Rufina was breast-feeding Maria Isabella when the officers who were trained at the School of the Americas invaded her village of El Mozote, which means The Thistle. When those men came in, they tore her little baby from her breast and they threw little Maria Isabel up in the air and bayoneted her.

Rufina, by the grace of God, was the only one who was able to survive that massacre. She hid behind a tree and prayed to her God that he would protect her so she could tell the story. As it says in the Bible, "I alone have escaped to tell you." And yet, just as happens with my own daughter, her breasts filled with milk but her baby was dead. And what pain for her, not only in her heart but in her body, in her breasts.

In the time of Herod, the innocent children were killed when Herod was looking for Jesus. And those mothers cried, too. They wept for their children, but their children were no more.

I represent Rufina in this court. Rufina has not had a court of justice to come to, and I feel all of us are really very honored to be able to stand here and to speak for those who are part of our family in Central America. When you're young, you have your family of birth and then you have your own children, and you have your extended family. But the finger of God draws a larger family for you when you get older, and God calls you to be minister to other people on earth, not just your own children. So we represent those who have suffered so much in Central America. We are called to represent them.

Of the 12 officers cited by the UN Truth Commission in 1993 for the murder of Rufina's children and the other 900 in El Mozote, of those 12 officers, ten of them were graduates of the School of the Americas. The bayoneting death of little Maria Isabella was a crime against humanity under Principle 6 of the Nuremberg Conventions.

I stand here honored to be able to witness for this little baby and her brother and her sisters. And I believe that justice will come and that the School of the Americas will be closed. We join our dreams with the dreams of Martin Luther King, the dreams for all children. We come from a God who asks us to live our life not just for ourselves, but for our larger family, calls us to love himself/herself, and to love our brothers and sisters.

I stand honored to be in this court with my fellow defendants, with this wonderful team who have defended us so eloquently, with this team of prosecution who are also very good-hearted, and with this judge who has lived through so much of history. We are grateful to be here. We are the grandmothers who walk into the future, grateful to God, thankful and rejoicing.

Solidarity Without Borders: The Witness of Hospitality

Interview with Laura Sánchez

One of the sources of solidarity that has been practiced for the past 150 years in the United States—particularly since the United States annexed over half of Mexico to its national territory—is the people-to-people solidarity offered to undocumented immigrants from Mexico, and later from Central America. This solidarity was given high visibility during the 1980s with the Sanctuary Movement, and it continues today, recalling the words of Emma Lazarus inscribed on the Statue of Liberty: "Keep, ancient lands, your storied pomp! Give me your tired, your poor, your huddled masses yearning to breathe free, the wretched refuse of your teeming shore. Send these, the homeless, tempest-tossed, to me; I lift my lamb beside the golden door."
Laura Sánchez is a community activist and director of Proyecto Hospitalidad in San Antonio, Texas. During the 1980s she opened her home to hundreds of Central American refugees and their families, and helped many of them apply for political asylum in Canada. Dennis Dunleavy shares excerpts from his interview with Laura in December 1997.

During the 1980s, as the darkness of civil war gripped many Central American countries, hundreds of thousands of refugees fled north through Mexico and into the United States. In Nicaragua, *Contra* guerrillas with the backing of the US government waged a covert war against the Sandinistas, while in Guatemala, more than 440 villages and as many as 75,000 people were killed in military counterinsurgency campaigns by 1985. In El Salvador, thousands fled a repressive military supported almost entirely with US tax dollars.

Many refugees, as they came north, were treated with suspicion and discrimination, and were subjected to arrest and deportation. For example,

214

by the end of the war in El Salvador less than 2 percent of all Salvadoran refugees in the US had obtained legal status through the political asylum process. As a result many people went underground, blending into the inner cities of Latino barrios in California and across the Southwest.

Grappling with the injustice of US foreign policy, many people of faith and justice opened their hearts to the new arrivals. Citing an affront to human dignity and basic human rights, the people of the Sanctuary Movement challenged the established "Cold War" dogma of the Reagan and Bush administrations. Reminiscent of Harriet Tubman's underground railroad to free slaves, thousands of Central Americans made their way into sanctuary safe houses in the United States or on to political asylum in Canada.

One woman in San Antonio, Texas who has dedicated her life to offering hospitality to the poor and oppressed from Latin America is Laura Sánchez. Over the years, Laura's faith, humility and perseverance has inspired many, and provided a deeper spiritual insight into the meaning of faith-based service. Since the early 1980s, Laura along with her husband Marcos and their daughters have assisted hundreds of refugees fleeing oppression and economic hardships in Latin America.

Laura's house, not far from the "cradle of the Texas Republic," the Alamo, is a busy place on a quiet street. Despite political and economic adversity, a feeling of calm prevails over the daily stream of crises and concerns. There is also an extraordinary sense that Laura's work goes well beyond simple acts of charity and reflects a spiritual path of healing and understanding for the human condition.

Toward the back of the main house a small converted garage serves as a sort of hostel for immigrants, many of whom have been injured from train or car accidents during their journeys north. Inside the cottage, along with the several bunk beds that line the walls, there is a small kitchen and a bathroom that is shared among the refugees.

Across from the cottage, a small chapel of plain unpainted wood is filled with wooden benches. On one wall, a hand-carved cross hangs surrounded by drawings of the passion of Christ. For many years, on Thursday nights, the refugees would gather for prayer and the reading of the Word. On these occasions, amongst friends, lessons from the wars would emerge. Accounts of leaving loved ones behind, or having to bury mothers, sons, and children, were brought to light. During the time shared in San Antonio, the long and difficult process of healing the body and the soul had begun.

Hospitality has always been a part of Laura's life. Shortly after World War II she remembers watching her grandmother waiting on lines at the American Consulate in Mexico.

It got started as a family tradition I guess. My grandmother helped people in Mexico as she learned the process for visas to the United States helping to bring my father's family back to Texas.

Born in San Luis Potosí, Mexico, Laura moved to San Antonio as a young girl with her family and quickly developed a strong faith relationship with God. In kindergarten, even though she spoke only Spanish, she recalls listening with attention to the lessons about serving others that she was taught in Catholic school.

I had somehow developed a relationship with Jesus at a very early age. I understood the love coming from Sister Gertrude and I had already put it together—this is what my father and mother did; this is what they gave to us and this is what God gives to us.

Even though they were very poor, Laura's family never turned away anyone who came to their home for help. As a young child in the late 1940s and early 1950s, Laura remembers men coming to the door with the simple plea of, *"un taquito por el amor de Dios."*

That is what they would say to my mother—One taco for the love of God—I remember that very clearly. Somehow the word spread amongst them that they could come to a particular house and they would not go away empty handed. My mother always gave of what we had.

For Laura, the charity at home impacted her deeply and provided the inspiration for her later work.

I saw the suffering of others in my own surrounding as I was growing up, even before the refugees from Central America started to come here. I saw the suffering not of my own family but of those that touched my family. I learned very distinctly the fine line between good and evil, and that we are responsible for ourselves and that we are responsible for each other and you are your brother's keeper. And if you do have two coats, one belongs to your brother or your sister that does not have one.

After a few years of factory work, Laura's father took the family to California to work as migrant workers.

We became migrant farm workers—I didn't know what we were doing, I just knew that we started working in the fields. It was really heart-breaking if you were an adult, but to us kids it was just one tremendous adventure. I remember one of the first places where asked to stay talk about the Posada and no place at the inn. When they saw my father coming with nine kids they closed their doors. We finally rented a chicken coop for a dollar a person per day.

At age twelve, Laura came to realize a terrible truth about the US attitude towards migrant farm workers.

I had come to love the United States and understand the Pledge of Allegiance. I had believed in it with all my heart growing up, but after meeting the Mexican national farm workers called braceros *who picked crops for less pay, it was not true. I could not understand why these men worked so hard. I asked why they never took breaks and they said they couldn't, because when you (US workers) are getting paid 2 cents a pound for string beans they were getting paid one cent a pound.*

The injustice experienced in the fields of California provoked, in Laura, an uncomfortable truth about her new homeland, the United States.

The Pledge of Allegiance became a fragment of lies because it was not true. "Liberty and Justice for all" meant the worst injustice and the worst oppression toward these men that were the braceros. They were my country people and that I think became the beginning of my advocacy.

With civil wars breaking out in Central America called upon people of faith to examine their convictions in more meaningful ways. Recalling summers she spent in Monterey, Mexico with her grandmother presenting the family's visa case to the consul, Laura decided to become involved with the refugees. She helped to organize what the Mennonites later called the "Overground Railroad" to Canada for Central American refugees.

This was in 1981, I did all of the terms that one needs to get a visa: filling our the applications, doing the interviews, translations, getting the police clearance, getting all the letters. We received the first twenty young Salvadoran men out of the El Coralón detention center and our work just mushroomed. We were the first shelter for refugees from Central America in San Antonio.

Working through the Canadian government, Laura sought alternatives to the US immigration policy by obtaining political asylum status for refugees outside the country. In Canada, dozens of Central Americans were given a chance to rebuild their lives away from the devastating violence and poverty at home.

One young woman, Ana Estela Guevara of El Salvador, met Laura while in detention in the Rio Grande Valley of Texas. After accusations by the military that she was a guerrilla commander, the FBI investigated the case and she was held on a $10,000 bond. Money was raised for court costs and eventually Guevara became part of the first group from San Antonio to receive political asylum in Canada.

As the legal proceedings later showed, the charges against her came not from connections to the rebels but from her association with the Emanuel Baptist Church in El Salvador and for carrying a Bible and some progressive music into the United States.

Another woman, María Lopez Castellanos, had a different story. As the mother of seven young children, María worked in a Guatemala soap factory for $1.50 a day. In 1987, she left the country to look for work in the United States in the hope that she could better support her children. While riding a train north across the border between the United States and Mexico, María slipped and fell beneath the wheels. Near death and separated from the four-year-daughter she was traveling with, she was placed in a hospital where surgeons amputated both legs below the knees.

Upon hearing of María's plight, Laura and others raised more than $16,000 to pay for her medical care, and eventually, with the help of the Catholic Church, found a small home for her in San Antonio. Reunited with her daughter, María began a long and arduous recovery. Her dreams of supporting her family in Guatemala soon vanished, but the compassion and dedication of those caring for her brought renewed hope—one that would help her to some day walk again.

It is not only the human condition that has been the focus of Laura's work, but also the struggle against the role the United States has played in maintaining the many structural inequalities which are built into the political, social and economic systems of countries in which the immigrants leave.

According to Laura, the southern part of our hemisphere has suffered tremendous economic and political oppression by the United States.

To me, it is the fact that it is not politics dictating the economy—it is the economics dictating the politics—and it is more and more that big business is saying what the government should and should not do.

Despite the wars in Central America having ended, many of the root causes of the conflicts remain: poverty, corruption, interference from foreign powers, unemployment and violence.

The war took place and El Salvador is still going through this same situation. That's why we still see people coming up. You don't see any real remedies in terms of the root problems. The root problems continue to be the economic situation of their country. It is very painful to realize that so much blood was shed and yet the changes that came about are not great.

In other ways, however, the lives of the people Laura has touched over the years have changed. Many refugees have become better educated and have broken through the cycle of poverty that has kept them from flourishing in their homelands. They have been touched by someone who has provided a humble shelter from which to escape the terrible storm of war and oppression.

For Laura, it is all an expression of faith and love for humanity.

God wants a life in abundance for all of us. That is one of the things I feel in my heart and I know in my soul, and in my mind that She has created enough for all of us to have what we need. Life in abundance is what He has given us, but we want more than abundance for ourselves and we don't want to share that.

Never considering all the risks of the work she was called to do, Laura's trust in the Creator has allowed her to become a voice for the voiceless:

When God called, since he had done all of this preparation, he had literally taken me by the hand and prepared me to know exactly what I needed to know when the time was ready for me to go into action.

Today, despite health concerns, Laura remains active with refugee and immigrant rights in Texas, and rarely does a day pass without the less fortunate of the world appearing at her doorsteps recalling the words of her youth, *"un taquito por el amor de Dios."*

Moral Imperatives For The World Bank

from the Religious Working Group on the World Bank and IMF

In recent years, the World Bank and the International Monetary Fund (IMF) have come under severe criticism from Third World countries and NGOs for requiring poor countries to radically restructure their economies in order to provide foreign exchange to pay their debt obligations to Northern creditors and international financial institutions. According to a declaration made by NGOs at the Fourth United Nations Conference on Women at Beijing in 1995, the structural adjustment programs of the World Bank and the IMF are "traumatizing whole continents, tearing apart the social fabric of entire societies, and wreaking havoc on the lives of billions of people worldwide, especially women."
The Religious Working Group on the World Bank and the IMF is a Washington-based coalition with representatives of more than 40 Protestant denominations and agencies, Catholic institutions and religious orders, and faith-based organizations working to build a broad network of people of faith active on issues of global economic justice. The following declaration incorporates "moral imperatives" to guide the economic decisions of the World Bank and the IMF that profoundly impact the lives of the poor throughout the world.

Economic decisions—by individuals, institutions and governments—involve moral choices and are subject to moral accountability. We recognize that it is a challenging task to apply moral values to one's institutional responsibilities. Yet our faith traditions insist that public policies be shaped and evaluated according to the standards of God's love and mandate of justice.

In the early 1980s many nations in the global South faced financial crisis. While there were many reasons why this situation developed, the immediate cause was unpayable debt service, precipitated by tight money policies in the rich countries that drastically hiked international interest rates. Much of the original debt was incurred in the 1970s by largely undemocratic governments through questionable lending practices by Northern banks. People living in poverty did not benefit from many of these loans, yet they bear the burden of repayment. In addition, they live with the effects of far-reaching economic policy changes required of countries to qualify for debt restructuring, new loans and foreign investment.

Termed "structural adjustment" and "economic reform," these policies have sought to control inflation and stimulate growth. They include devaluing the national currency; raising interest rates and decreasing the availability of credit; reducing government spending—usually resulting in deep cuts in social programs and subsidies; lowering tariffs and liberalizing trade; and selling state-owned enterprises. Agricultural and industrial production is shifted from food staples and basic goods for domestic use to commodities for export. Adjustment prescriptions have been designed by international institutions led by rich nations and implemented by debtor governments without popular debate or civil society participation.

Poverty, Suffering, Injustice and Discrimination

Adjustment has profound consequences for people in the global South and their natural environments. We hear from brothers and sisters around the world that conditions for many people living in poverty and suffering under injustice and discrimination have worsened as the result of these measures.

We recognized that some kind of economic reform is often necessary and that environmentally responsible growth is important for impoverished countries. But it is morally unacceptable that people who struggle bravely to survive are carrying the burden of these policies on the assumption that the benefits may eventually "trickle down." Means as well as ends must be just. In addition, some evidence suggests that the long-term results of current adjustment policies may be the consignment of millions of people to permanent deprivation. We urge international financial institutions and governments to seek new approaches, which involve greater openness and flexibility, foster broader civil society participation, protect the environment and encourage more equitable distribution of economic power and resources within and among nations.

We Make the Road By Walking

We write as people of faith in the United States. In listening to our Southern colleagues and reflecting on our faith traditions, we have put forth a set of moral criteria applicable to the design and evaluation of economic reforms. We offer these principles as a basis for dialogue, conscious that as individuals and religious institutions we, too, need to make new efforts to embrace more fully the values we articulate.

The values we affirm here are not new. They are rooted in our Scriptures and have been expressed repeatedly in our churches' public statements on social, economic and environmental justice. While this statement is explicit about our underlying theological convictions derived from the Christian tradition, we understand that other religious faiths and widely accepted moral beliefs embrace similar values. Each section of this statement presents a biblical/theological affirmation, applies this as a moral standard to economic reform measures and summarizes what we have seen and heard about the current reality.

All Life Exists Within the Sphere of God's Care and Judgment

Individuals, institutions, business enterprises and governments are objects of God's concern and subject to moral accountability. This includes the economic realm. There are no economic "laws" that can place policy decisions beyond moral scrutiny. Economic actors and policymakers are morally accountable for their choices and their effects, intended or otherwise, on people and all of God's creation. Since "the earth is God's," its resources must be employed in a sustainable manner for the benefit of all, not just a privileged minority.

To be just, economic reform measures must contribute to a social framework in which property ownership and use, productive activity and commerce occur at a level and in a manner suitable for meeting the basic needs of all, serving the common good, alleviating poverty and preserving the natural environment.

In practice, we have seen and heard that economic adjustment measures have made it more difficult for many people to meet their basic needs and often result in environmental damage. We observe that policies supported by appeals to inevitability, efficiency and aggregate growth often have had the effect of serving the interests of the wealthy and powerful at the expense of ordinary people. International institutions, governments and private corporations frequently focus on their short term institutional benefit, failing to serve the common good adequately.

Human Beings Are Created in the Image of God

All persons—male and female—are created in the divine image, loved by God and equal in worth, dignity and fundamental rights. Bearing the divine image, everyone has the right and responsibility to participate meaningfully in the political, social and economic decisions that shape their society. In harmony with all creation, all people are entitled to an equitable share in the fruits of the earth. The economy exists for people, not people for the economy.

To be just, economic reform measures must respect and enhance human dignity and gender equity. They must be flexibly designed and implemented with the consent of the people expressed through authentically participatory and democratic processes. Reforms must be held accountable to international human rights standards and treaties.

In practice, we have seen and heard that the nature and pace of adjustment measures generally have been determined without public debate or civil society participation. We observe that, as a result, some persons who enjoy political, social and economic privileges benefit from these policies, while many of those who lack such privileges are compelled to carry the principal burden of adjustment, having to cope on a daily basis with its negative consequences. We see and hear that adjustment has too often contributed to the weakening of human rights, for example, by placing additional burdens disproportionately on women, who often must increase their unpaid and paid labor to make up for the loss of government services and family income.

Human Beings Are Persons-in-Community, Intended to Live in Relationships of Human Solidarity According to the Norms of Love and Justice

All people are created and called to love God and neighbor—across the divisions of ethnicity, class and nation. Justice is love distributed and requires that everyone have access to sufficient resources to live in dignity, meet their family's needs and fully participate in the shared life of their community. Great extremes in the distribution of income and wealth must be avoided. Our relationship with God and one another is violated when some people have much more than they need while many others lack the basic necessities.

To be just, economic reform measures must promote a more equitable distribution of power and wealth within and among nations. Reform must foster solidarity and justice among people locally, regionally and internationally, reduce economic and social inequality, and support and strengthen local communities and cooperative development processes.

In practice, we have seen and heard that economic adjustment has often resulted in greater unemployment, decreasing wages and deteriorating working conditions for many, while increasing the wealth of some. We observe that the pattern of wealth distribution in the global, national and local economies is generally becoming more skewed, and that reforms have not addressed this injustice. We have seen and heard that this accelerating inequality has weakened families and communities.

God Is Redeemer and Liberator, Calling Us to a Special Concern for People Living in Poverty and Oppression

The work of God involves lifting up and empowering people living in poverty and the redemption of human beings from every kind of oppression, personal and social. According to Christ's teaching in Matthew 25, nations and people will be judged on the basis of how they treat the hungry, homeless and most vulnerable members of society. Public policies, laws and economic relationships that we create can become instruments of emancipation by giving preference to the dignity of labor, human rights, gender equality and sustaining the earth above the interests of capital.

To be just, economic reform measures must make poverty eradication the priority for every phase of reform. Reform must not increase the burden on the poorest members of society, but should maximize benefits and minimize costs for all categories of people living in poverty. It must ensure that people struggling to overcome poverty have access to productive assets, benefit from public and private investment, and are served by the generation of sustainable livelihoods. Reform must recognize the role of the state and other forces of society to appropriately control the market and provide a social safety net.

In practice, we have seen and heard that even when macroeconomic indicators suggest improvement in a country's economy, people living in poverty frequently experience increasing insecurity and see insufficiency deepen into misery. For example, a country's overall agricultural sector can be growing because of exports by commercial farms, even as small farmers lose the ability to make a simple living. We observe that adjustment measures have often resulted in dramatic decreases in social spending, recent attempts to mitigate social damage notwithstanding. We see that the unpaid work of women—often made more burdensome by structural adjustment—is not even included in official economic indicators. We observe that reforms often have created a climate in which labor rights are difficult to exercise and where people in poverty must compete with each other for their means of survival.

Creation Is an Expression of the Goodness of the Creator and Is Endowed with Dignity and Value.

Human beings are called to live in mutually sustaining relationships with each other and with all creation. Human activity should enhance, not destroy, the beauty, diversity and richness of all life. The unsustainable use of increasing portions of the earth's resources deprives people and all God's creatures of what the Creator has provided: enough for all. In response to God's work of reconciling all things in Christ, human beings are called to repentance for abusing the earth and to the restoration of their broken relationships with all creation.

To be just, economic reform measures must promote sustainable development. Reforms must be designed to improve the quality of human life, preserve the natural environment, respect all creatures and ensure the ability of future generations to meet their own spiritual and material needs.

In practice, we have seen and heard that economic reform measures too often have had the effect of accelerating soil degradation, water pollution, watershed disruption, the destruction of critical habitat and the loss of other renewable and nonrenewable natural resources. We see that reform has often weakened governments' ability to protect the environment. We observe that the need for growth in impoverished countries must be balanced by worldwide efforts to end environmentally unsustainable production and consumption, especially in the industrialized countries.

Sin Is Social and Institutional, As Well As Personal

Social sin is present where there are growing economic disparities, increasing concentrations of economic power, and accelerating environmental abuse. Only God is ultimate. It is a form of idolatry when any given economic model or system is viewed as complete or fully adequate.

To be just, economic reform measures must not be rigidly based on any one economic model. They should be flexibly adapted to specific social, economic and environmental contexts and open to innovative designs responsive to popular and democratic needs and initiatives.

In practice, we have seen and heard much skepticism from people living in and struggling to overcome poverty concerning the current economic model that emphasizes minimal government, "trickle down" and global integration. We observe that adjustment measures based on this model have not adequately taken into account individual countries' particular sets of needs and circumstances or to the social and environmental consequences of such reforms.

All Humanity Is Called to Forgiveness, Reconciliation and Jubilee

The biblical witness mandates just and equitable commercial relationships, selfless help to those in need and the cancellation of oppressive debts that keep people locked in poverty. It calls for the restoration of land and livelihood to the dispossessed. Jesus taught that God will treat our debts in light of our treatment of others' debts to us. The crushing international debt burden unjustly carried by millions of people living in impoverished countries cries out for justice.

To be just, economic reform measures must be accompanied by a definitive cancellation of the crushing international debt of poor countries. Debt relief must not be rigidly conditioned on adjustment that further burdens people living in poverty, and it must be implemented in ways that primarily benefit the ordinary people who have borne the major burden of their countries' indebtedness.

In practice, we have seen and heard that entire economies are reshaped by the conditions placed on debt restructuring and new loans. While international creditors have now acknowledged that unsustainable debt burdens should be relieved, current strategies have set mere "debt sustainability" as their stated goal. Even if this approach is successful, people living in poverty will be left perpetually repaying resource-draining debts. We observe that the real goal of debt relief and economic reform must be socially and environmentally sustainable development within the framework of just and equitable global relationships.

Proclaiming
The Year
Of Jubilee:
Freedom From Debt

by Marie Dennis

In the year 2000, the churches of the world will celebrate a Jubilee Year, harking back to the Hebrew Scriptures. In the Jubilee Year social inequalities are rectified: slaves are freed, land is returned to original owners, and debts are cancelled. For the poorest nations of the world, the Jubilee Year holds out great promise. Between 1980 and 1990, the Latin American debt increased from $250 billion to $450 billion—even after paying $285 billion in debt payments to Northern creditors and international financial institutions during that same time period. The debt is clearly crushing the poor in Third World countries, and diverting valuable foreign exchange earnings to pay interest on the debt. According to Oxfam International, "Debt repayments have meant health centers without drugs and trained staff, schools without basic teaching equipment, and the collapse of agricultural extension services."

In this final reflection on the meaning of the Jubilee Year for the nations of the world, Marie Dennis offers the perspective of people of faith and religious groups joined in global efforts of solidarity—such as the Religious Working Group on the World Bank and the IMF, and the Jubilee 2000 Campaign—to cancel the foreign debt. She is the Director of the Maryknoll Office for Global Concerns in Washington, DC and New York. This reflection appeared in the Fall 1995 edition of Challenge, *EPICA's quarterly magazine.*

The closing decade of the twentieth century has thus far presented one occasion after another for retelling the stories of our peoples, for examining the signs of the times, and for testing our faithfulness—our authenticity—as followers of the Word. As if to prepare us for a dramatic entry into the third millennium we have been challenged to reflect as perhaps never before on who we are, where we are going, how we will get there, and with which companions we will travel.

We Make the Road By Walking

Those of us for whom the biblical image of Jubilee has meaning have been impressed by the powerful symbolism of the fiftieth years: 50 years times ten since Columbus arrived in the Americas; 50 years since the dawn of the nuclear age; 50 years since the end of World War II; 50 years since the founding of the United Nations; 50 years of existence for the World Bank and the International Monetary Fund (IMF).

Jubilee Happens When We Have Lost Our Vision

By definition, Jubilee happens when there are wrongs to right, injustices to correct, alienations to heal, brokenness to repair. Jubilee happens when we forget who we are as people and communities. Jubilee happens when we have lost the vision and our way.

These have been years of searching for new solutions to regional and global problems. One glance at the state and work of the United Nations in its fiftieth year suggests most clearly the scope of the transformation we are yet called to effect. While it attempts to stop aggression and negotiate peace; monitor human rights and accompany processes of demilitarization; care for the world's children, refugee populations, and indigenous peoples, the United Nations yet struggles under the burden of an unrepresentative structure and decision-making processes at the highest level. In this decade UN-sponsored conferences and summit meetings have gathered citizens and governments to address global concerns, including ecology, population, social development, and women.

Energized by the concern of citizens around the world, but hampered by political intrigue and power-mongering, these gatherings produced voluminous words in carefully crafted documents that only occasionally bear fruit in program or policy or patterns of human behavior.

As a civilization we are working our way through profound challenges to our own value systems. Each localized example of injustice and oppression in our world, we have come to realize, is supported by systemic level injustice and powerful worldviews that have tragically thus far prevailed.

The Voice of Women Cries Out in Beijing

We see sexism and injustice against women continuing, but we hear the voices of women that are stronger and clearer and more articulate every day. The vibrant participation of women from around the world in the United Nations Conference in Beijing was an excellent example. The clarification of an agenda that would eliminate some of the systemic prejudices and injustices against half of the human race is a sign of hope. Whether the meeting in Beijing was effective in terms of public policy or not, surely it was a demonstration of the determination, passion, energy, creativity, and intelligence of the women who gathered there and the millions they represented.

In these years we are celebrating the fact that more and more essential decisions about our work toward Jubilee are being made in concert with partners around the world; that leadership in the global movement against systems of repression and injustice is increasingly coming from the world of the poor and from women. Jubilee would see the melodious crescendo of women's voices heard and celebrated. Literally.

Also in this decade, the 50th anniversary of the nuclear age and of the end of World War II evoked a memory so painful that too often it generated anger and defensiveness instead of repentance and reparation. It is a memory—not only a memory but about the now as well—of nuclear nations unwilling to agree to meaningful denuclearization—of economies dependent on the arms trade—of land mines planted where children play—of money spent for death rather than life. Jubilee would see seeds of peace, seeds of life replacing seeds of death, an end to the terror of the nuclear age, an end to the global arms bazaar. Literally.

Earlier in this decade, the Quincentenary of the Europeans' arrival in this hemisphere forced us to acknowledge racism, genocide, the desecration of sacred place, and the abuse of peoples, their land, their honored traditions. Jubilee would see an end to racism, slaves freed, land returned in the Americas. Literally.

Approaching the New Millennium

As the new millennium approaches, the poor majority of our world know in their souls that the global economy is not functioning on their behalf. They experience the violences of hunger and illiteracy and disease in the fabric of their lives. They share a sliver of the world's wealth with millions of others while the extreme minority who are wealthy wield power over their lives.

In response, an amazing global network of very capable and serious women and men are working to change this system. Of necessity they are joining efforts with women's organizations, as women are the first to suffer in an unjust economy, as well as with those striving for ecological justice and an end to environmentally destructive models of "development."

Challenges to economic institutions and their decision-making processes are taking place in every major international arena, from the United Nations Social Development Summit in Copenhagen, to the meeting of the G-7 nations in Halifax, to the UN Conference on Women in Beijing, to the annual meetings of the World Bank and International Monetary Fund (IMF) in Washington, DC.

Of particular concern are the heavy debt burdens devastating impoverished peoples and their communities. In these years of fiftieth anniversaries, as we move toward the millennium, a global movement for deep reform of the international financial institutions, including the World Bank and the IMF, is emerging. Jubilee would see debts that keep whole nations in bondage forgiven—many labelled "already paid." Literally.

Witnessing a New Paradigm Shift

Some have described these last years of the twentieth century as witnessing a paradigm shift. It is a period of time that will be remembered as a major fault line in history, the close of the so-called modern era. Early in this decade, a multi-cultural, faith-based partnership of local communities and groups in the United States launched a process of reflection and discernment to articulate the signs of crisis in our US society and our world.

Written in the tradition of the Kairos Documents from South Africa, Central America, and many other nations of the impoverished Southern Hemisphere, Kairos USA agonized over the "systemic injustice and perverse values, social evil and personal irresponsibilities" that "permeate the fabric of our lives." Painfully aware of the ten "fiftieth years" that have passed without Jubilee in the Americas, the Kairos USA document, however, also identified opportunities for creative response from communities of faith to the crises of our times—articulated in the language of Jubilee:

"As provocative spark to the imagination, we recognize in this *kairos* a jubilean time. We look to the sabbatical legislation for hints and clues and root assumptions:

The earth is the Lord's.

The earth shall rest.

Debt is slavery.

You were freed.

Jesus is herald of the Jubilee-*kairos*.

In the fullness of his own time, Jesus proclaims the reign and realm of God—vibrant with the jubilee spirit. Its signs are the forgiveness of debt, release from captivity, from denials of all varieties, from sin itself. The contours of Jubilee are yet to be defined, but the invitation is clear and the need is great.

-On the Way: From Kairos to Jubilee, Kairos USA

Epilogue

We Make
The Road
By Walking

The Subversive
And Joyful
Memory
Of The Martyrs

by Jon Sobrino, S.J.

Before his death in 1989, Jesuit martyr Ignacio Ellacuria spoke of "the crucified peoples of the Americas." The poor reveal to us today the meaning of the cross to our faith, because they bear the weight of social and economic policies that exclude and oppress them. In a similar vein another martyr, Archbishop Oscar Romero, said that the poor "tell us what the world is really like, and what the mission of the Church should be." Where, then, is the hope? Precisely in those who remember the witness of the martyrs and take it to heart, bearing the cross they bore and struggling as they did to create a world in which the poor have life and dignity. In so doing, we shall truly make our own the wisdom of the early Church: "The blood of the martyrs is the seed on new Christians." In this epilogue, Jesuit theologian Jon Sobrino offers us a reflection on the subversive and joyous memory of the martyrs. He is the Director of the Oscar Romero Pastoral Center. This reflection appeared in the July 1994 edition of "Letter to the Churches," published by the Central American University (UCA) in San Salvador and translated by CRISPAZ.

The well-known German theologian, Johannes Baptist Metz, popularized the expression "subversive memory" in order to rediscover the true Jesus, as opposed to a saccharine Jesus, or an abstract Jesus that one can choose to believe in or not. The most radical way to recover the subversive element of that memory consists in remembering that Jesus ended up crucified on a cross, a memory that in this post-modern world is either not taken seriously or considered to be in bad taste.

Perhaps the most profound reason why we do not confront that subversive memory is that the cross subverts the lie and unmasks the truth: the "truth" of a society in the time of Jesus and in our own time, the "truth" of state socialism and neoliberal capitalism. "What Europe has is fear," is how Ignacio Ellacuria described it, at a conference in Barcelona in 1989. It is as though the world is afraid of the truth, believing it is better to forget the cross of Jesus because it reminds us of death and sin—words increasingly remote in our language, and a concept that we no longer talk about.

I should like to clarify that the fundamental problem is not whether or not one believes in Jesus, but whether or not we accept our complicity in producing crosses—the cross of Golgotha, of Bosnia, of Haiti. Here in El Salvador, we know this very well. The generals and the colonels accused of horrendous crimes have insisted on "forgiveness and forgetting," hoping to eradicate memory because memory is subversive. What is at stake in the recollection of memory is actually the will to face the truth.

To Give the Very Best of Ourselves

In Latin America, we have also insisted on a "joyful memory" of Jesus who is Good News and who is at the same time, God, human being and Savior. It is the memory of Jesus who went about doing good, who did not come to be served but to serve, who began one of his most famous discourses with the words, "Blessed are you." Jesus truly loved those human beings joyfully: he welcomed the marginalized, cured the sick, consoled the afflicted. Through all of this, Jesus wished us to give the very best of ourselves.

However, it is profoundly difficult to retain the joy of this memory. The greatest difficulty is not in the acceptance that in Jesus "the compassion of God appeared" divinely, but rather in the hubris in which we prefer to decide for ourselves what joy and goodness are and what it is that makes us human. Therefore, the memory of the best of Jesus disappears, that which all the world might understand, whether they be believers or not: the parables of the Prodigal Son, the Good Samaritan, the Final Judgment, the rich man Epulon and the poor man Lazarus, the Sermon on the Mount, the Our Father prayer.

And the memory of Jesus' great love disappears: he gave his life to defend the poor, the weak and the vulnerable, and "loved them to the end." In the absence of the joyful memory the spirit to do good disappears, and the problem then is whether or not we have a willingness to be kind, to do good and to be open to receive kindness in return.

Finally, it must be said that the subversive and joyful memory is just that—memory. It has come down to us through tradition, it has been given to us. It may well be that post-modern theory or the daily desire to "live as well as possible" is not interested in memory. However, the Christian must accept that all begins with the crucified and resurrected Jesus and that without that living memory—and without putting it into practice—there is no Christianity, regardless of the many orthodoxies, rituals and canons. What is at stake is opening ourselves to the gift of grace.

The Crosses of Crucified Peoples in History

The most specific portion of this memory continues to be the cross of the assassinated and martyred Jesus, the darkness and light, the sin and grace. From that point on, true Christianity will be nothing else but bringing people and societies together against the part of the cross that is sin, and in support of the part of the cross that is love. Undoubtedly, there are many things that Christians will have to do and rethink, from ecology to pastoral orientation, but what they may never ignore is the cross.

For the person who has the will to be true and good, with an openness to the gift of grace, it will not be difficult to find. Neither should it be difficult to kneel before the cross and kiss it as is done during Holy Week. It is there that we find the crucified ones in Rwanda, Haiti, Bosnia; the poverty in Nicaragua, Bangladesh, Chad.

Here in El Salvador we do not forget the cross. In El Mozote and Las Aradas, near the Sumpul River, there are monuments in remembrance of the victims of both massacres. In the chapel of the Divine Providence Hospital there is a plaque in memory of Monsignor Romero. A short distance from my office is the place where the Jesuits were assassinated, along with Julia Elba and Celina. Someone had the good idea to turn it into a garden. The exuberance of our tropical climate and the dedication of our gardener, Obdulio—Julia Elba's husband and Celina's father—caused the roses to flower. "Red roses for the Jesuits and yellow roses for the my wife and daughter," Obdulio would say.

I have seen thousands of people come to this garden as though they were entering St. Peter's Basilica in Rome. El Mozote, Las Aradas, the Divine Providence Hospital chapel, and the rose garden at the UCA all cause trembling—they give you shivers, provoking silence, respect and tears from the visitors. Likewise, they have an element of fascination—something that attracts and brings to light the best that each of us has within. For that reason, I believe the rose garden produces roses that are better than they were when they were planted. They carry within them more light and hope.

The Subversive and Joyous Memory of the Martyrs

In this way, the martyrs of El Salvador—and of our entire continent—continue the subversive and joyous memory that Jesus of Nazareth began, maintaining a tradition that evokes what is most human in all of us. It exhorts us to live more for one another and provokes us to a commitment to truth, peace and justice. It compels us to be more human. It maintains hope in the midst of so much disenchantment.

Another European theologian, Jurgen Moltmann, says, "Not all life gives hope, but the life of Jesus does; the Jesus who gave his life on the cross out of love." Not all people are reason for hope, but there is hope in the men and women who have shown that love is possible. They have demonstrated a profound love by giving their lives for others, even in a world of institutionalized egoism.

Here in the Oscar Romero Pastoral Center at the Central American University (UCA), we are attempting several things: theological reflection, instruction, publications, liturgies, pastoral work. But above all, we want to be "custodians of the holy places," to keep alive the subversive and joyous memory of the martyrs. Ignacio Ellacuria had the audacity to say, "With Monsignor Romero, God came to El Salvador." Many of us believe that this is true and not just with Monsignor Romero, but that God also came through the Rutilios and Celinas.

History changes, clearly, but without keeping alive the subversive and joyful memory of God's arrival to us, we will be walking down the wrong path into the future. Conversely, if we keep that memory in our presence—of Jesus and of the martyrs—then kindness and gentleness, service and compassion, truth and justice will continue to be a possibility and a reality in our midst.